MW01143661

Managing Your Business to Its Maximum Sales Potential

by

James F. O'Hara

Copyright © 2004 by James F. O'Hara

ISBN 0-7414-2097-X

Published by:

1094 *New DeHaven Street, Suite 100*
West Conshohocken, PA 19428-2713
Info@buybooksontheweb.com
www.buybooksontheweb.com
Toll-free (877) BUY BOOK
Local Phone (610) 941-9999
Fax (610) 941-9959

Printed in the United States of America

Printed on Recycled Paper

Published October 2004

To Karen, my loving wife and the light in my life and to my mother, Peg, whose love and commitment is embedded on every page of this book.

Table of Contents

"Only those who risk going too far can possibly
find out how far one can go."

T. S. Eliot

Foreword

I've always been intrigued by the almost reverential status we bestow on abstract thinkers. Despite the fact we usually don't fully understand what they're saying, we feel a need to elevate them to royalty. As you go through this book, I'm confident you won't be burdened by any such feelings.

This book is a commonsense, realistic guide for managing the internal organization of a business, any business, so that it can reach its full sales potential. It might just as easily been entitled, "A Manager's Guide to Getting Your Business Out of Its Own Way."

Throughout my career, I've had the pleasure of working for four of America's most respected corporations. Even within these fine organizations, conditions existed that guaranteed none of them would ever realize its maximum sales or earnings potential.

Like most people, I too wasted tremendous amounts of time trying to navigate around the seemingly endless parade of company-created obstacles that served no purpose other than limit everyone's productivity. I just accepted them as part of the normal workday. For years, I did this unquestioningly until one day I realized the extent to which these situations were undermining my performance and the performance of the company.

I wasn't the only one being affected. Looking around, it was obvious that everyone in the organization was being forced to contend with the same obstacles.

There had to be a better way! I decided to find it and share it with others. This Program, *Managing Your Business to Its Maximum Sales Potential,* is the product of those efforts.

The paradox of adequate performance standards is in its self-deception. We convince ourselves we're performing at our highest possible level of achievement, when we're actually capable of so much more.

The Author

Overview

"The greatest warrior conquers himself first."

Robert Pater,

"Leading from Within."

Without even realizing it, businesses routinely leave between 20% and 30% of their potential sales in the marketplace. In other words, for every $1 million in sales they are getting, they're leaving an additional $200,000 to $300,000 on the street!

These lost sales aren't the result of external factors such as increased competition or changing technologies. The sales I'm referring to are being lost to conditions that exist within the companies themselves; factors over which they have direct control.

You see, as productive as most companies are, they're also repositories for inefficiency. Anyone who's ever held a job knows only too well the many innovative ways their own companies can tie up their time with unproductive pursuits. Rarely, however, do we stop to consider the costs of these situations in terms of lost earnings.

Just imagine how sales and earnings would improve if companies eliminated these inefficiencies and directed all of their energy and resources into revenue-generating activities. We no longer have to imagine. *Managing Your Business to Its Maximum Sales Potential* provides a step-by-step plan for doing just that.

This book has been years in the making – thirty-five to be exact. Over that period, I've held a variety of sales and sales management positions with four world-class organizations.

i

In addition to my firsthand view of these companies, my work has given me the opportunity to observe hundreds of others of all shapes, sizes and industries.

Like most in Sales, my primary focus had always been on the external factors affecting my performance. I paid little attention to the demands being made by my own company. Nothing, however, exposes weaknesses more tellingly than adversity. As the economy started to decline, I began looking more closely at how companies, particularly my own, were responding to the challenge.

To my great disappointment, I found most of my company's responses to be merely cosmetic with little chance of actually improving performance. In fact, we often seemed to be doing just the opposite of what was needed. Instead of constructive action and much needed support, the demands for non-selling activities increased. Worse yet, our selling strategies were constantly being revised. One month margin improvement was all the rage only to be replaced by market share or collections the next. Hope, rather than experience and informed planning, was the basis for most decisions.

Not only were we responding inappropriately to the demands of a difficult economic climate, but we were competing with ourselves. The inside staff was being yanked every which way, politics dominated much of the decision-making, policies became more inflexible and management continued to assign responsibility for the company's sales performance exclusively to the Sales Department.

They say that the greatest forces for success or failure must come from within. As individuals, we must first conquer ourselves, if we're ever going to reach our full potential. The same is true of business organizations. Every business organization must eliminate, or at least minimize, its internal weaknesses before it is realistically prepared to face the challenges of the marketplace.

As the conduit between the company and the marketplace, the Sales Department is particularly vulnerable to any internal weaknesses. In fact, few poor sales performances are the result of factors occurring within Sales. More often than not, they're caused by internal factors such as office politics, unnecessary administrative burdens or cultural issues. These conditions which I classify as inefficiencies are present in every business organization. Unfortunately, their role in affecting sales performance is frequently underestimated or ignored.

Only the most astute managers truly appreciate the link that exists between a company's internal operations and its sales performance. When sales don't meet expectations, most almost instinctively look to the Sales Department for the cause. Little attention is paid to any other segment of the business.

This misplaced blame inevitably leads to the procession of fruitless remedies I call the *MORES: more* salespeople, *more* sales calls, *more* reports, *more* territorial realignments, *more* tracking of sales activities, and *more* training. The company ends up with *more* of everything except sales.

Inefficiencies can always be traced back to other more global weaknesses within a business. For example, excessive or unnecessary procedures are most prevalent in highly political cultures and poor communications always plays a prominent role in high turnover. To conquer the inefficiency, we must first address these underlying causes.

In business, as in life, we tend to focus on symptoms. We reach for an aspirin to lower a fever which only returns if the illness itself hasn't been cured. In business, alleviating the symptoms without curing the illness only ensures the cycle of underperformance will continue.

Managing Your Business to Its Maximum Sales Potential is designed to address both the symptoms and the illness. The Program consists of two separate, yet cooperative, initiatives. One is aimed at modifying or eliminating those internal situations that are wasting resources and energy, while the other addresses the conditions within the company's framework that are causing them. This dual approach is intended to first put the organization on the road to reaching its maximum sales potential and then keeping it there.

There are already a number of programs designed to improve business efficiency. The *Maximum Sales Potential* Program is the only one, however, that focuses exclusively on sales growth as the measure of its success. This doesn't mean sales at any cost. All sales growth must be accompanied by maintaining and even improving current margin levels.

This isn't a book on sales techniques. It's strictly a guide for leading a business to its full sales potential. As such, the target audience is business executives and managers.

The Program is presented in three parts. Part I, **Maximum Sales: The Most Logical Goal,** consists of four segments stressing the irrefutable realities of business, namely: the constancy of change, the unrivaled importance of sales to the health of every business, the gap between adequate and maximum sales performance and identifying ways that companies commonly waste valuable energy and resources.

Part II, **The Twelve Attributes for Maximum Sales**, dedicates one chapter to each quality to be integrated into the organization's framework. Each segment ends with a questionnaire designed to provide the reader with a clear understanding of the importance of that particular Attribute to the sales success of their company.

Part III, **The Implementation**, consists of only one segment detailing each step involved in the adoption and implementtation of the Program.

Losing to a competitor is a shame; however, beating yourself is foolishness. Companies, nonetheless, continue to sacrifice a tremendous volume of their sales to conditions over which they have direct control.

Individually, most inefficiencies do little damage. Cumulatively, however, they can lead to a death by a thousand cuts. In picking up this book you've taken the first major step toward stopping the bleeding.

PART I

MAXIMUM SALES:

THE MOST LOGICAL GOAL

"Change is the law of life. Those who look only to the past or the present are certain to miss the future."

John F. Kennedy

Chapter 1

Change Is Not a Choice

*"Even if you're on the right track, you'll get run over
if you just sit there."*
Will Rogers

To appreciate the forces of change, we need only look at some of the earth-shattering technological advances that have taken place just over the past twenty years. Startling advances such as cell phones, the internet and fiber optics allow us to communicate instantly, while acronyms such as WiFi, DNA and MRI are understood throughout the world.

The changes in business have been equally remarkable. Corporations that had been household names have literally disappeared into the endless abyss of mergers and acquisitions. Once revolutionary concepts such as telecommuting, family leave and medical savings accounts are now standard.

Prior to 1980, Americans often spent their entire career with a single company. Today, they work for an average of eight during their careers. The 401(k) has displaced the pension as the primary retirement plan and the Personnel Department has been replaced by the more ornate Human Resources.

Changes in the demographics of workers have been equally dramatic. Today's workforce is more diverse and more complex than ever. Just twenty years ago, management was almost exclusively white and male, while full medical coverage and tuition reimbursement were standard benefits. Today, female and other minority managers and executives are commonplace, medical costs are shared and educational benefits are virtually nonexistent.

Attitudes and expectations have also changed. Workers are now far more independent. Their focus is on short term, personal gain and they freely admit to placing personal interests over those of the company. Not too long ago, voicing such attitudes would have been blasphemy.

These changes are not without a price. There is now a substantial distance between the companies and their employees. Blindly following the dictates of corporate leadership is a thing of the past. The rash of layoffs in response to the recent economic downturn has only validated the widely held belief that companies have little allegiance to their workers. Allegations of improprieties by top executives of Enron, WorldCom, Parmalat, Global Crossing, HealthSouth and others have further contributed to this erosion in worker loyalty.

Clearly, management is operating in a minefield. On one hand, it's enjoying advances in productivity never dreamed possible. On the other, it faces what is arguably the most complex and demanding workforce in history.

Handled incorrectly, this potentially explosive situation can result in a workforce totally alienated from management and disinterested in the success of the company. In such a setting, the *status quo* becomes the ideal and workers have little interest in embracing change. Stagnation is never far behind.

This mindset increases the risks in an already risky world. Michael Dell, Chairman and CEO of the Dell Corporation describes the situation this way, "If you accept the *status quo* as 'good enough,' you're managing in the rearview mirror. In this economy, you can bet you'll end up smashing right into the future. Just to stay competitive, you have to constantly question everything you do." [1]

4

You see, in business, change isn't a choice. Regardless of its size or industry, every company must be continuously changing to remain competitive. The consequences for not keeping up with the times are clearly evident on the following list of former winners of the prestigious Malcolm Baldrige Award that have suffered serious reversals in their fortunes.

NAT'L. INSTITUE OF STANDARDS TECHNOLOGY
2002 MALCOLM BALDRIGE AWARD RECIPIENTS*

DATE OF AWARD	COMPANY	STOCK PRICE AT TIME OF AWARD	RECENT STOCK PRICE
11/92	Lucent	$44.12	$ 3.17
11/92	Texas Instruments	$49.37	$20.03
11/94	AT&T Consumer.	$54.50	$14.78
11/95	Corning	$25.75	$10.26
11/95	Armstrong Industries.	$58.88	$ 1.35
11/97	Solectron	$40.87	$ 5.22
11/97	Xerox	$79.87	$13.53

*Source: www.nist.gov/public_affairs/factsheet/SPchart.htm

Unlike golf, business doesn't give mulligans. As any company on this list can attest, all it takes is a simple lapse in judgment to be toppled from a position of dominance. The failure to respond quickly or effectively to changing customer preferences, changing technologies, changing demographics, or any other critical changes can bring down even the most established company. Regardless of past successes, businesses are in a state of constant vulnerability.

"Tomorrow is being made today."

Peter Drucker

My first fulltime job was with the Bulova Watch Company. At the time, Bulova was the premier manufacturer of timepieces in the world. The name Bulova was synonymous with excellence. Its Accutron™, the world's first electronic timepiece, placed it atop the industry.

Without warning, a new technology, quartz, arrived on the scene. Trusting the Accutron™ would assure its position, Bulova chose not to pursue this new technology. Seiko, on the other hand, did and the rest is history. As quickly as you can say, "we should have been less complacent," Seiko emerged as the new industry leader, while Bulova became just another footnote in the history of American business.

Only recently, forty years after that fateful decision, have I once again seen a Bulova commercial. Because of one bad decision, the fortunes of a once great company were reversed for over two generations. A similar fate awaits any business that fails to respond to the changes in the marketplace.

Microsoft almost fell prey to a similar lapse in judgment. By his own admission, Bill Gates made the potentially fatal mistake of underestimating the power and popularity of the internet. Only a speedy reversal of his decision and accelerated investments by Microsoft have enabled it to establish itself as a competitive force in this pervasive technology.

Not to be overlooked is Bill Gates' acknowledgement of his error in judgment. Rarely, are mistakes accompanied by such public admissions. His admission was the meaningful first step in limiting the damage.

The magnitude and adoptability of technological advances in virtually every industry eliminates all other options. If a company is to compete, it has no choice but to be a proactive participant. The growth of the internet clearly illustrates this point.

This one technology has literally revolutionized the entire business landscape. It has drastically increased competition by lowering barriers-to-entry, while enabling new businesses to compete on par with long-established ones. By making it easy for customers to comparison shop, it has also made it very difficult for companies to raise prices.

Could anyone have foreseen the day when retailers without stores like Amazon, eBay and Books-a-Million would have sales in the billions of dollars, while those with stores would generate over 30% of their sales to customers they've never seen?

In fairness, no one could have truly predicted the massive impact it would have. One thing was certain, however, the longer a company delayed embracing it, the greater its risk of lost market share and eroded margins.

Many new opportunities began to evolve as the internet gained acceptance. Transcending its original purpose as an information source, it soon began providing opportunities to substantially lower costs. Companies established their own websites and started using them for many of their customer services and ordering activities. The resulting cost savings have enabled them to remain competitive in a very difficult environment.

As with all revolutionary advances, new and exciting uses have emerged. For example, businesses have found more and more innovative ways to transfer duties to the customer. Self-service gas stations, ATM's and automatic checkouts at the supermarket are now everywhere. In fact, we've become so accepting of the speed and convenience they provide that we avoid businesses that don't provide them.

It doesn't stop there. Federal Express and UPS now track every package throughout the delivery process. By providing immediate tracking information on their websites, these companies have improved the quality of their service, while lowering their need for support personnel.

Companies also now save on paper, handling and postage costs by sending bills and order information electronically. Immediate and accurate management of inventory is the norm. Inventory replenishment in most companies is now totally hands-free. Stock trades are completed immediately. Research that formerly took days is now completed in just a couple of clicks of a mouse.

The benefits are not limited to cost savings or service quality. The information companies now gather on their customers is priceless. In an instant, they know who their customers are, where they live and what they buy. This enables them to manage inventory more effectively, read changing trends more quickly and better meet the needs and wants of those customers.

The allure of hanging on to what's currently working is always enticing. This middle of the road philosophy can easily mislead us into believing we're avoiding unnecessary risks. But, as they say in Texas, the only things in the middle of the road are yellow lines and dead armadillos. The greatest risks aren't in changing, but in not changing.

Every leader would be well served to heed the warning, "If your business isn't growing, you're dying."[2]   You can't manage for tomorrow by clinging to today; current methods and philosophies must be challenged. To reap the rewards of any opportunity, a business must be alert, flexible and have a culture that welcomes change. *Managing Your Business to Its Maximum Potential* will instill those attributes into the very core of a business organization.

"If earnings growth supplies the engine,
rising sales provide the fuel."

Monica Tija
Investors Business Daily

Chapter 2

Sales: The Most Important Priority

"You can't shrink your way to greatness."
Tom Peters

One aspect of management that no business leader can ever afford to lose sight of is the absolute importance of sales to the health of their business. It seems that every time a company announces that it has missed its earnings target, the culprit is always "lower than expected sales." This should serve as proof positive of the direct link that exists between every company's sales performance and its success.

When I was in the Air Force, our sole mission was to defend America from the air. All activities and personnel were dedicated to supporting that single mission. Regardless of whether we had the best hospitals, the most advanced computer systems or the finest administrators, if the aircraft and aircrews couldn't respond to any threat to our national security, we had failed.

This is no different than sales performance is to a business. "Looking at a company's sales figures can give you a peek into the heart of its business. At its most basic level, the business of a business is selling a product or service." [3]

Sales are the financial foundation on which every business is built. Every position in a business organization is created for the purpose of supporting its sales performance. Think about it. If a company didn't have sales, it wouldn't need an Accounts Receivable Department since there wouldn't be any money to collect. Customer Service would also be unnecessary since there would be no customers to serve and Human Resources would also be expendable since there

11

wouldn't be a reason to hire anyone. Businesses exist to make money and for every business, its primary source for revenues and profits is always sales.

According to Robert Whitney, co-author of *The New Psychology of Persuasion and Motivation in Selling*, "The average American salesman keeps 33 men and women at work...and is responsible for the livelihood of 130 people."[4] I'm not sure I agree with the ratios, but the link Mr. Whitney establishes between sales performance and jobs is clearly evidenced by the consistent change in the unemployment rate that accompanies every change in the economy.

The net income of every business is derived from sales. In it's simplest form, the formula for determining earnings is:

Gross Sales x Gross Margin % – Expenses = Net Income

This suggests that a business can grow by some variation of increasing sales, raising margins, or lowering expenses. No business, however, wants to rely on either increased margins or controlling expenses for its success.

Legendary fund manager, John Neff, explains it this way: "My style of security analysis examines earnings and sales: (1) earnings growth drives the P/E and the stock price, and (2) dividends come from earnings. Ultimately, *growing sales create growing earnings*. Squeezing greater earnings from each dollar of sales (called margin improvement) can buttress a case for investing, but margins do not grow to the sky. Eventually, attractive companies must demonstrate sales growth." [5]

Have you ever heard of anyone losing his or her job because they sold too much? Picture a scenario where the boss says, "What are you trying to do, put us out of business? You sold our entire inventory. You're fired!" I don't think so. All too often, however, we read that benignly worded press release stating that people are being laid off due to "revenue shortfalls." Translation, "Sales are down. You're fired."

The bull market of the 90's was an anomaly. It was also a testimony to the absolute power of sales. Every three months, we held our collective breaths in anticipation of corporate earnings announcements. Like football and baseball, we now even have an earnings season. Fortunes and jobs are won and lost on each company's announcement.

To fully appreciate the impact of sales on earnings, we need only compare the stock prices and media coverage of companies at the height of the bull market to those made just one year later after the downturn of the economy. Consider some of these examples:

The EMC Corporation reported a 50 percent jump in earnings yesterday . . . EMC shares rose $3.81 to $83.06.
(New York Times, July 20, 2000, pC4, col. 4)

*EMC shares closed down $8.43 to $21.60 – a year low – as 49.6 million shares changed hands . . . The stock is off 67.5% this year, erasing some $100 billion in shareholder value... The EPS shortfall indicates that hardware pricing, volume shipments and software **sales fell precipitously** below expectations.*
Reuters, July 6, 2001 - 5:13 PM ET)

In a move widely anticipated by financial analysts, Intel Corp. has announced a 2-for-1 stock split . . . Investors greeted the news by bidding Intel up $4.44 to $137.19
(The Bergen Record, Jan. 29, 1999, pB3)

*Intel reported ...revenue would rise 3 to 5 percent. Analysts had been predicting growth of 12 to 15 percent. The reason for the slowdown in revenue . . . **slump in sales.** Intel finished the day at $47.94 . . . down $13.55.*
(New York Times, Sept. 23, 2000, pC1(L) col 05)

13

*Intel Corp., the world's largest maker of computer chips, announced yesterday that it is cutting 5,000 jobs . . . Intel had announced in January that **sales for its first quarter would drop about 15%** from the previous quarter, but now the company said the decline likely will be 25 %.*
(The Washington Post, March 9, 2001, pE01)

*Sun Microsystems reported **sales rose 42 percent** to $5.02 billion . . . shares rose $4.12 to $98.06.*
(New York Times, July 21, 2000, pC2(L) col 01)

*Sun Microsystems said yesterday . . . it will **fall well short of projected sales** and earnings in the current quarter. Sun tumbles as low as $18.81 in after-hours trading.*
(New York Times, Feb. 23, 2001 pC1(L) col 05)

Cisco at $65.50 . . . sales rose 60% from $3.56 billion to $5.72 billion.
(The Times (London, England), Aug. 9, 2000, p.22)

Cisco fell . . . to $12.35 . . . predicted a weaker second quarter due to soft sales.
(The Bergen Record, Nov. 8, 2002, p. B02)

This relationship between sales and stock valuation is historically consistent. As sales performance improves, stock values increase. Correspondingly, as it declines, stock values follow suit.

The rule of business is brutally uncompromising: the trip down is appreciably faster and less enjoyable than the trip up. If you want to experience true loneliness, just be the CEO of a company when it misses its quarterly number. You'll quickly understand the true meaning of the adage, *"Victory finds a hundred fathers, but defeat is an orphan."* [6]

"Missing the number," is the Wall Street euphemism for insufficient sales. Sales performance is seen as a key barometer of organizational and managerial prowess by the investment community. Failure to meet sales expectations is viewed as impotence. Wall Street will forgive a lapse in earnings due to one-time charges or a large investment for future growth, but it is relentlessly unforgiving of lower than expected sales.

It's truly a "what have you done for me lately" world. For even the most successful executives, the journey from the cover of <u>Fortune</u> to being the answer to the trivia question, "Whatever happened to _____" is just a few bad quarters away. Consider the odyssey of Eckhard Pfeiffer of Compaq Computer. In 1998, he was hailed as one of the darlings of the technology industry. He was on the cover of the June issue of <u>Selling Power</u> under the headline, "How Eckhard Pfeiffer is propelling Compaq toward $50 billion in sales." [7]

Just one year later, he was run out of town on a rail. What happened? Did Mr. Pfeiffer lose his leadership abilities overnight? No, he missed his number. More accurately, Compaq's sales performance failed to meet expectations.

Companies can literally undersell themselves into obscurity. Does anyone recall Osborne Computer, maker of the first portable business computer? Would you like a few tickets to a World Football League game? What about the World Hockey Association? Let's go over to Burger Chef for a bite to eat. The examples are endless. For every company that makes it, thousands fail and insufficient sales is always at the root of those failures.

Even great companies aren't immune. Procter & Gamble's shares dropped $20 the day it announced it would miss its earnings estimates because of lower than expected sales. It has since regained its luster due primarily to, you guessed it, improved sales performance.

Lucent, once the most widely held stock in the world, plummeted from $62.98 to an abysmal $1.50 due to declining sales, while Hewlett Packard took the giant slalom from $68.09 to $16.00 for the same reason. Fortunately, the stock prices of both these companies have started to rebound in concert with their improving sales results. Once again, the direct link between sales performance and company success is affirmed.

When asked if their company is committed to attaining maximum sales, most CEOs respond emphatically in the affirmative. This, however, is more often wishful thinking than reality. Even as they make their proclamations, their companies are routinely squandering energy and resources.

This isn't to say that there aren't many solid sales organizations; well-managed companies with records of consistent sales growth. Even with the most successful of companies, there's always a substantial gap between the sales levels they attain and the sales levels they're capable of attaining.

There's a wide variety of reasons why companies allow this to happen. Those reasons can be operational, psychological or cultural in nature. Reasons aside, we can be sure of one thing: the self-inflicted loss of sales revenues can be reversed. That's the objective of *Managing Your Business to its Maximum Sales Potential*.

In the next chapter, we'll explore the difference between the adequate performance standards under which most businesses operate and the maximum performance levels they're capable of attaining.

"Any man who selects a goal in life which can be fully achieved has already defined his own limitations."

Cavett Robert
American Speaker & Writer

Chapter 3

Adequate vs. Maximum Performance

"People say they can't succeed and spend the rest of their lives proving it."

Jean Nidetch
Founder, Weight Watchers

Exactly what is a company's *Maximum Sales Potential*? Simply stated, it's the highest level of sales that can be attained with the resources it has invested. A business can only reach its maximum potential when all of those resources are being fully and effectively utilized in pursuit of that one goal.

Unfortunately, most companies aren't even aware of their full capabilities because they're so accepting of adequate performance. In fact, adequate performance is very often mistaken for maximum performance.

Except for sports, American society places amazingly little emphasis on striving for maximum performance. In fact, actual performance is frequently treated cosmetically to give the appearance of excellence. Just look at the shenanigans that have taken place in our schools. Manipulation of grades is so prevalent that high grades no longer represent academic achievement. The format for scoring SAT tests was actually changed in 1996. The change, not surprisingly, resulted in a substantial inflation of scores.

In its 1983 report, "The Nation at Risk," the National Commission on Excellence in Education proclaimed, "If an unfriendly foreign power ever attempted to impose on America the mediocre educational performance that exists today, we might have used it as an act of war. As it stands,

19

we have allowed this to happen to ourselves."[8]   That was over twenty years ago and by all indications the situation hasn't improved.

Not only has adequate performance been elevated, there are mechanisms in place designed specifically to minimize superior achievement.   Let's look at our Asian-American students. Collectively, they represent the highest achievers in America's schools.   More than any group, they understand the demands inherent in realizing the American dream and pursue it without pleas for diminished standards.

Based on their record, you would think that their formula for academic success would be adopted as the prototype for all of American education. Instead, this success gets minimized by the educational elite who attribute it to intense pressures exerted at home.

This trend is not confined to any one discipline or segment of society. We see it everywhere from the government to the workplace. It's not how you perform, it's how you appear to perform.

Why has adequate performance become so widely accepted? Quite simply, it provides the illusion of accomplishment at a discounted price. In a nutshell, it's a bargain!

The price of success is not lost to everyone. Rafe Esquith, a Los Angeles elementary school teacher, understands it and guides his students accordingly. Hanging across the front of his classroom is a banner proclaiming, "There are no shortcuts." He understands that learning isn't easy nor should it be.

All of his students want the good life. They would also like to get it while, like electricity, following the path of least resistance. Esquith, however, will have none of that. He constantly stresses to them, "We aren't handed happiness. We're given an opportunity to pursue it."[9]

His record speaks for itself. With students from a part of Los Angeles where violence is the norm and English is a second language, Esquith's students consistently "score in the country's top 10 percent on standardized tests and go to colleges such as Harvard, Princeton . . . and Stanford." [10]

The same tendencies Rafe Esquith fights to overcome in his classroom are prevalent throughout the business world. We all want to follow the path of least resistance and we all tend to dress up our own performance to appear like our maximum potential. Leadership, however, must determine the standards of performance that will apply.

The standard formula for calculating sales quotas illustrates how adequate performance becomes the standard. At the end of each year, management takes the sales performance for the current year, increases it by the requisite ten or fifteen percent and – *voila!* – we have next year's quota. Economic conditions, product quality, the internal capabilities of the company and all other factors aside, the performance benchmark for the coming year has now been established. Whether we're capable of producing more is never even a consideration.

Like so many rituals and accepted myths in business, sales quotas are a game – an exercise in performance limitations. In assigning quotas, management believes it is establishing minimal performance expectations for each salesperson. To the recipient, however, quotas are most often seen as performance ceilings.

I've always been amused at the way quotas affect behaviors. Once they reach the magic number, salespeople strut around the office with an expression of confidence; secure in the knowledge they're safe for another year. They assume the air of the good team player as they feign concern for those unfortunate souls still mired in the depths of under-quota depression. Meanwhile, the latter group walks around with furrowed brows searching out any opportunities that might also deliver them to the safe harbor of adequate performance.

Businesses should take a lesson from the flea. An interesting phenomenon takes place when a flea is placed in a covered jar. When the lid is removed, the flea never again jumps higher than the top of the jar - a prisoner of its own expectations.

With their expectations, executives and managers often put a lid on their own companies. Their expectations can serve as either a ceiling or a floor. As a ceiling, minimal growth will most certainly result. As a floor, however, the chances for accelerated growth markedly improve.

Setting expectations shouldn't be viewed as an incidental event in a business. Expectations have been scientifically proven to be a viable performance predictor. Known as the Pygmalion effect, Robert Rosenthal of the University of California describes it this way, "Expectation becomes a self-fulfilling prophesy. When teachers have been led to expect better intellectual performance from their students, they tend to get it. When coaches are led to expect better athletic performance from their athletes, they tend to get it. When researchers are led to expect a certain response from their research subjects, they tend to get it." [11]

If expectations affect performance, why would any executives or managers have limited expectations of the same people they have hired and trained? Aren't these the same individuals in whom they've entrusted the success or failure of the company? It seems far more logical that their expectations be geared towards maximum performance.

I wonder what would happen if a company chose to forego preset performance goals and dedicated its efforts to maximum performance each day. For Al Arbour, coach of the New York Islander dynasty of the 1980's, excellence was the standard. He expected maximum effort at all times and his players knew it. It was his belief that shifts add up to periods, periods to games, and games to seasons. The net result was four consecutive Stanley Cup championships.

I believe excellence is the external manifestation of internal commitment. There were players who jumped higher and ran faster, yet Michael Jordan dominated his sport. All professional golfers strike the ball beautifully, yet Tiger Woods consistently dominates. Their peers actually speak in awe of their accomplishments. What we see in each of these individuals is the externalization of their inner strengths – the fulfillment of their expectations of themselves.

Businesses aren't any different. Maximum performance for a business organization requires the same internal commitment. Every company's level of achievement is determined by its own internal strengths and expectations. One of management's primary responsibilities then is to infuse into each member of the organization a belief in and commitment to reaching their full individual and collective potential.

In the case of maximum achievers like Arbour, Jordan and Woods, the difference between their actual achievement and their maximum potential is appreciably less than the 20% - 30% performance gap under which most individuals and companies operate. Closing that gap is the objective of this Program.

The positive effects of enthusiasm should also not be underestimated in this pursuit. Mary Kay, founder of the cosmetics empire bearing her name, always understood this. She'd tell everyone within earshot, "Act enthusiastic and you'll be enthusiastic. Nothing great was ever accomplished without enthusiasm." [12] As the individuals responsible for leading the organization, managers must demonstrate enthusiasm and consistently stress this message to their employees.

The process of *Managing Your Business to Its Maximum Sales Potential* is designed to lift all boats by raising the water level throughout a company. Once adopted, it will dramatically improve the work environment and employee job satisfaction by fostering both individual and company growth.

There is an inverse relationship between the successful adoption of this Program and the width of the gap between a company's actual sales performance and its maximum sales potential. The gap between the two will narrow in response to the energy and enthusiasm generated by this Program.

Pretty Good

by

Charles Osgood

There once was a pretty good student,
Who sat in a pretty good class;
Who was taught by a pretty good teacher,
Who always let pretty good pass –

He wasn't terrific at reading
He wasn't a whizbang at math;
But for him education was leading
Straight down a pretty good path.

He didn't find school too exciting,
But he wanted to do pretty well;
And he did have some trouble with writing,
And no one had taught him to spell.

When doing arithmetic problems,
Pretty good was regarded as fine –
5 plus 5 needn't always add up to be 10
A pretty good answer was 9.

The pretty good class that he sat in
Was part of a pretty good school;
And the student was not the exception,
On the contrary, he was the rule.

The pretty good student, in fact, was
Part of a pretty good mob;
And the first time he knew that he lacked was
When he looked for a pretty good job.

It was then, when he sought a position,
He discovered that life could be tough-
And he soon had a sneaking suspicion,
Pretty good might not be good enough.

The pretty good town in our story
Was part of a pretty good state,
Which had pretty good aspirations,
And prayed for a pretty good fate.

There once was a pretty good nation,
Pretty proud of the greatness it had,
Which learned much too late, if you want to be great,
Pretty good is, in fact, pretty bad. *

* Printed in <u>There Are No Shortcuts</u> by Rafe Esquith

Inefficiency – diverting resources away from productive activities to unproductive ones.

The Author

Chapter 4

Know the Enemy: Identifying Inefficiencies

"So much of what we call management consists in making it difficult for people to work."
Peter Drucker

The time has come for us to identify some of the dragons we intend to slay.

When we think of inefficiencies, we usually limit ourselves to the more common ones such as competition between departments, unnecessary meetings or the unending requests for reports. These represent only a small percentage of the internal situations that divert time and energy away from productive endeavors.

As long as employees feel estranged from the company and don't have a financial stake in its performance, there will never be a shortage of ways they'll find to make themselves and others less productive. Although the volume of inefficiencies may differ between companies, there isn't a business anywhere that isn't operating <u>below</u> its full capabilities.

Before we can even think of correcting these problems, we must first unearth their actual causes. To help in this effort, I've compiled the following list of factors that are the source of many of the inefficiencies.

As you review the list, you'll find you're familiar with most of them. That's fine since these are the primary factors that must be addressed if your company is to fulfill its maximum potential. The factors to consider include:

Cultural Impact:

Nothing influences a company's performance more than its culture. A company's culture dictates how individuals and departments interact, what type of behavior is acceptable, the degree to which politics influences activities and all the other factors comprising its internal environment and priorities.

It also determines the degree to which inefficiencies will be tolerated. For example, a culture emphasizing productivity and performance is less apt to adopt unproductive activities than one dominated by politics. In light of its global influence within the organization, the impact of culture on performance must never be overlooked.

Inappropriate Assignment of Authority:

Occasionally, management will delegate responsibilities to individuals who have neither the experience nor skills to effectively handle them. When this happens, inefficiencies are sure to result.

One instance comes to mind. I worked with a person whose performance and attitude actually warranted disciplinary action. Customers complained, co-workers avoided dealing with her and she was overtly adversarial to Sales. In lieu of taking appropriate action, management reassigned her to a new position. Unfortunately, in this new position, her approval was required on critical, time-sensitive processes. Before long, she was holding everyone hostage and giving approvals on the basis of whether she liked or didn't like the person making the request. The net result was unnecessary delays, time wasted and irate customers.

Poorly Designed Hiring Profile and Screening Process:

A key factor in determining performance is the quality of individuals being brought into the organization. To improve the odds for success, the Program recommends that a process be adopted requiring each candidate to successfully complete separate interviews with no less than three leaders prior to being hired. This should go a long way to minimizing the time lost, lowered morale and high turnover that result from mistakes in hiring.

Turnover:
The loss of productive employees is rife with hidden costs. Screening, interviewing, lost production, time, training and workload reassignments are but a few of the costs incurred when any productive worker leaves a company. Low turnover is such a critical element to the success of any business that it has been selected as Attribute #12 of this Program and is covered in detail in Part II of this book.

Poor or Nonexistent Communications:
How many problems would be averted and how much time would be saved, if people only communicated? In business, situations are always occurring that require effective communication. The failure to communicate events like the introduction of new policies or changes in procedures undermines performance by creating delays, confusion and internal conflict. It also compromises a company's image in the eyes of its customers.

Poor or nonexistent internal communications is a source for untold inefficiencies. It is, therefore, one of the key areas to be closely scrutinized when working to bring a business to its full performance potential.

> **"How well we communicate is determined not by how well we say things but by how well we're understood."**
>
> **Andrew Grove**
> "One On One With Andy Grove"
> **Former CEO, Intel Corp.**

Multiple Roles:

Inefficiencies always occur when individuals are expected to fulfill two separate roles. This frequently happens when Sales managers are asked to serve as both manager and salesperson. Their effectiveness is diminished in both roles and the company ends up with neither a salesperson nor a manager. To make matters worse, the salespeople must then work without the guidance of their leader. Multiple roles are always an inefficient use of personnel and a strategy that puts an unfair burden on both parties.

Failing to Take Action with Unproductive or Disruptive Employees:

The most upsetting responsibility facing any manager is probably reprimanding or terminating an employee. It is also one of the most important.

An unproductive or disruptive employee can upset the stability of an entire organization. For either political or personal reasons, managers sometimes will either allow the problem to persist or attempt to pass it off to another department. Not only is this unprofessional and dishonest, it undercuts productivity by allowing the inefficiencies created by this type of employee to continue unimpeded.

To avoid this situation, unproductive or disruptive workers must be dealt with by their current manager in a timely, effective manner.

Unnecessary or Redundant Forms:

Departments or individuals often develop forms that must be completed, signed and submitted before they will perform their assigned duty. In unproductive settings, this can serve as both a way to exert authority over other departments and a way to control the pace and volume of workloads. In all cases, unnecessary forms slow productivity and frustrate productive workers.

The National Account Group in one company to which I was affiliated required that a forty page form be completed before they would open an account. Filled with requirements for irrelevant information, the form literally took hours for each salesperson to complete and delayed the initiation of service to new national accounts.

All requests for a more reasonable version were denied.

Interestingly, the form remained long after the individual who created it had left the company. I'll bet that even now, years later, the same form is still in use and management remains befuddled by its consistent lack of sales growth.

Insufficient Staffing:

To control costs, managers sometimes choose to postpone or cancel the hiring of needed support personnel. This is like buying sneakers without the shoe laces. In every instance I've seen over the years, this strategy has resulted in diminished performance.

One of my customers had only one Administrator for a force of over fifty sales representatives. As you might imagine, a great deal of their selling time was diverted to performing administrative tasks. The costs in lost sales alone always exceed any savings realized by not hiring sufficient support personnel. When it comes to investing in needed support, such frugality is usually an indication of flawed judgment and shortsighted management.

Unclear Customer / Product Instructions:

Providing clear, understandable instructions is critically important to efficient operations. In addition to straining relations with customers, unclear instructions divert valuable time and resources away from productive activities as staff members must respond to customer calls for help. These costs can all be avoided simply by providing clear, user-friendly instructions.

> I recently purchased a brand name printer. When I needed to print in landscape format, I realized that option wasn't accessible in the printer's software. Worse yet, the manual made no mention of printing orientations.
>
> I called the company. After a fifteen minute wait, a representative explained the process. After complaining she got calls about this all the time, I recommended she make a suggestion that the manual be edited.
>
> Something as simple as unclear instructions can have far-reaching consequences like requiring additional staffing, straining customer loyalty and causing delays in response time for customer support.
>
> Isn't it foolish to manufacture a quality product and then sabotage your own success with a poorly written product manual?

Uncompetitive Compensation:

Operating "on the cheap" all but guarantees low productivity and high inefficiencies. When compensation is below market levels, employees perform with an indifference that creates delays and inferior work quality. For a business to compete, its compensation must be competitive. For a business to attain its maximum sales potential, its compensation must support that goal. Attribute #11 of this Program is specifically designed to satisfy this requirement.

Political Selection of Managers:

Promoting individuals on the basis of their political standing and not their experience and talents is a formula for wasted resources. Unless people in positions of leadership have the tools necessary to motivate and lead, the organization is setting itself up for failure.

Moving away from promotions based on merit has additional repercussions. It demeans the integrity of the selection process, lowers morale and creates internal conflicts. These are extremely high costs to pay for individuals who offer the company a lower return on its investment than other more deserving candidates.

I worked with a fellow who epitomized the adage, "all sizzle and no steak." He had all the packaging of a superstar without the record to support it.

High-profile projects, glad-handing, emails, this guy was right out of central casting. Despite his lackluster record, he was promoted to headquarters. What was to be his *coup de grâce,* however, turned out to be his Waterloo. His new manager saw right through all the fluff and fired him within a few months.

The damage he inflicted on the company, however, in terms of the time wasted, lowered morale and distrust of management lingers to this day.

Indifferent Orientation Process:

You don't get a second chance to make a first impression. The way companies welcome new employees is a critically important, yet frequently minimized, factor in determining performance. When a company fails to welcome its new members with enthusiasm and a sense of inclusion, it will be very hard pressed to build a cohesive environment.

Such an oversight lengthens the time before new employees are productive, while increasing the chances they'll leave the company prematurely.

Office Design and Support Materials:
Frequently overlooked time wasters are the design of the office and the storage location of commonly used support materials. Time spent traveling to key support areas is time taken from productive activities. In my last company, Sales was housed on a different floor than the Sales Administrator. Any interaction, therefore, meant going downstairs to the Administrator's station.

The location and availability of commonly used items such as catalogs, envelopes and postage can also consume substantial amounts of time. Once again, time spent chasing down such items is taken from other more productive uses.

On surface, this might seem like a minor issue. When you multiply the time required for each item by the total number of times the employees need them, the design of the office is no longer a trivial concern. It can, in fact, be a major waste of resources.

Annual Reviews:
At the risk of sounding blasphemous, I believe annual reviews are one of the most ineffective and costly rituals in business. Each year, managers spend days preparing written assessments on each employee. They then spend more time presenting these evaluations to the employee.

Psychologists know that the most effective time to provide feedback on a behavior is immediately after it occurs. This principle also applies to management. Unfortunately, the annual review process offers busy managers the option of postponing such communications. By mandating a formal schedule, it can also minimize the need for frequent communication with members of their department.

Eliminating the annual review would do the following:

- It would encourage frequent and ongoing communication between managers and employees

- It would eliminate the temptation to postpone addressing performance issues as soon as they occur

- Finally, it would eliminate the three to four week block of time spent each year as managers scurry to satisfy the employee review mandate, while trying to remember the events of the past twelve months.

This recommendation isn't meant to put an end to employee-management communications. To the contrary, the Program advocates more frequent communications without the time constraints inherent in the annual review process.

Managers would now be expected to communicate with each employee on a far more regular basis. This will provide each with opportunities to voice their concerns and preferences more regularly, thereby, improving both performance and morale.

This is by no means a complete list of all the internal factors that can affect the performance of a business. In reviewing this list, however, I'm sure you've recognized many as ones affecting your own company. Before any business can hope to reach its *Maximum Sales Potential*, it must modify and/or eliminate those situations that are keeping it from attaining that goal. A close examination of each of these factors within your company will reveal many of the inefficiencies that are keeping it from that goal.

PART II

THE TWELVE ATTRIBUTES
FOR MAXIMUM SALES

The Twelve Attributes:

The Organizational Qualities of a Sales Healthy Business

I   **Maximum Sales: The Only True Goal**

II   **Experienced, Qualified Leaders**

III   **Flexible and Embracing of Change**

IV   **Minimal Internal Politics**

V   **Sales-Friendly Culture**

VI   **Enjoyable Customer Experience**

VII   **Management is Responsible for Sales**

VIII   **Decisions are Made Holistically**

IX   **Full Costs are Always Considered**

X   **All Employees are Familiar with the Demands of Selling**

XI   **Compensation Structured for Sales Growth**

XII   **Low Turnover**

"The very essence of leadership is that you have to have a vision. It's got to be a vision you articulate clearly and forcefully on every occasion. You cannot blow an uncertain trumpet."

Theodore Hesburgh
President,
University of Notre Dame

Attribute #1

Maximum Sales: The Only True Goal

Imagine telling an airline ticket agent you'd like to buy a ticket to Europe. Of course, the agent will immediately need to know, "Where in Europe?" As ridiculous as this might sound, many businesses operate the same way - not knowing exactly what it is they're trying to accomplish.

The best kept secret in most business organizations is its primary objective; the thing the CEO most wants to accomplish. Whether it's called the objective, destination or goal is irrelevant. What is relevant is the need for every business to have one. A clearly defined and universally communicated objective is a critical element to the success of any endeavor – particularly one as competitive and complex as business. As Henry Thoreau so aptly put it, "In the long run, men hit only what they aim at."

Companies operating without a clearly defined objective are like ships without anchors; they're at the mercy of the elements. Like day traders, they jump from trend to trend in an endless search for the next quick fix. Unfortunately, this usually results in little more than a reshuffling of priorities and a further drain of company resources.

As its leader, the CEO is responsible for defining and communicating the company's objective. That objective then serves as both a motivator and a map for every employee. It must inform every employee of leadership's expectations and where their energies must be directed.

In addition to providing the employees with a direction for their efforts, a clearly stated objective defines the criteria against which the company will judge its own performance - its concept of success. With consistent reinforcement from management, every employee must direct all of their activities so they're contributing to that objective. Current activities not contributing to that objective must either be modified or eliminated, while any new ones must be shown to support achievement of that objective.

One of my pet peeves has always been the declaration of multiple objectives for a company. In an attempt to cover all the bases, CEOs feel required to present a shopping list of priorities. This is like inflicting Attention Deficit Disorder on an organization. The intended message gets diluted and the chances for success are greatly diminished.

I've always felt that businesses, like individuals, perform best when focused on a single, clearly defined objective. All the forces within a company must then direct their energies toward that one objective; greatly increasing the probability it will be attained. This Program requires maximum sales be established as the one, overriding objective for the entire organization.

"Management by objectives works if you know the objectives. Ninety percent of the time you don't.

Peter Drucker
Management Consultant

In his book, *Good to Great,* Jim Collins refers to Isaiah Berlin's essay, "The Hedgehog and the Fox," to illustrate this point. Day after day, the cunning, sleek fox is outwitted by the clumsy, unattractive hedgehog, who avoids becoming the fox's lunch by curling into a ball of painfully prickly bristles. The reason for the hedgehog's success is simple. "Foxes pursue many ends at the same time . . . never integrating their thinking into one overall concept or unifying vision. Hedgehogs, on the other hand, simplify a complex world into a single organizing idea, a basic principle or concept that unifies and guides everything." [13]

There are a number of mediums available to the CEOs to communicate a company's objective. The Mission Statement and Statement of Direction are the two most common.

When declaring the objective, the CEO must decide between the direct, unambiguous approach and the less direct, less risky one. The political safety of the latter prevails in far too many instances.

The net result is a succession of noncommittal, carefully-worded phrases intended more for display in the annual report than for providing the employees with a target for their energies. As doctors are taught, the objective seems to be, "First, do no harm." Those that opt for the safer approach, however, squander an excellent opportunity to improve the company's chances for success.

Here are a few examples of actual corporate statements that fall woefully short of declaring a clearly defined objective:

"To be the partner of choice for the world's leading service providers by helping them create, build and maintain the most cost-effective . . . networks . . ."

"We are a large and diverse community of individuals who trust and respect one another as we work to enhance the quality of life for people around the world."

"In meeting their (customers) needs everything we do must be of high quality. We must constantly strive to reduce our cost . . . Customers' orders must be serviced promptly and accurately . . . Our suppliers and distributors must have an opportunity to make a fair profit . . ."

"Deepening Relationships . . . Disciplined Growth . . . Execution and Innovation . . . Supporting Our Communities"

It's not that these messages say anything wrong. It's just that they don't say anything. After reading any of them, no employee would truly know where their company was going and what was expected of them. Amazingly, each of these is the statement of a Fortune 500 corporation.

> **"If you do not know where you are going, every road will get you nowhere."**
>
> **Henry Kissinger**
> U.S. Secretary of State

If a company is committed to reaching its maximum sales potential, its Statement of Direction should read something like this, "The XYZ Company is a sales organization. All of our energies, resources, and activities are dedicated to maximizing earnings by maximizing our sales performance."

The objective is clear, direct and understandable to everyone; particularly those who will make it a reality. A clearly defined, sales-focused objective is the critical first Attribute to be adopted in the process of *Managing Your Business to Its Maximum Sales Potential*.

As stated in the Overview, this is not an endorsement of price-generated sales growth. All sales growth must be accompanied by a commensurate growth in earnings.

As the Program matures within a company, efficiency in all critical disciplines will steadily improve. These improved efficiencies will translate into improved services for the customers. These improved efficiencies will provide greater pricing latitude which, in turn, will lead to the expected profit growth.

This progression of improved efficiencies leading to earnings growth is really the ultimate objective of this Program. You see, in establishing *Maximum Sales* as the goal for the entire organization, the CEO is in actuality driving the business to its *maximum earnings potential*.

Attribute #1 Questionnaire

What's your company's primary objective? _____
_____

Does it have a formal Mission Statement? _____

If yes, who prepared it? _____

If no, how do employees know the company goals?
_____

**Do employees receive regular updates on the company's
financial performance?** _____

Are there always a lot of rumors going around? _____

What's the single greatest threat facing the company?
_____

How does the CEO communicate with the employees?
_____

**Do people and departments work cooperatively or compete
with one another?** _____

Why do you think that is? _____
_____

Is everyone working towards the same goal? _____

**Do you think a clearly defined objective would improve
company performance?** _____
Explain? _____
_____

"The productivity of work is not the responsibility of the worker but of the manager."

Peter Drucker
Managing in Turbulent Times

Attribute #2

Experienced, Qualified Leaders

When you need surgery, you wouldn't think of looking for a doctor who's just out of medical school anymore than you would board a plane piloted by someone who just received their flying license. Yes indeed, we rely on experience as one of the most accurate predictors of performance.

Football coaches always lament, "They make so many rookie mistakes." What they're really saying is that players lacking in actual game experience are far more prone to error than those who have it.

> **"You cannot create experience. You must undergo it.**
> **Albert Camus**

The same principle applies to executives and managers. There aren't any guarantees in business, however, the chances for success can certainly be increased by only selecting individuals with the aptitude, attitude and experience for leadership roles.

Have you ever noticed how vividly you remember the best manager you ever had? Think back over your years. What traits did they have that made such an impression on you?

I'll always remember the respectful way Mickey Mantle shared his memories of his first professional manager, Harry Craft. In his autobiography, *The Education of a Baseball Player,* Mantle recalled, "He was the man, next to my father, whom I wanted most to be like. He taught me many things about baseball but he also taught me many more things about being a man. . . . It seemed to me that Harry Craft always looked the part of a manager or a leader. He was always friendly but dignified, stern but not sour and he walked like a man who knew where he was going and what he was going to do when he got there." [14]

Talk about a lasting impression, Mantle wrote this glowing tribute in 1969, nineteen years after he played for Craft.

I've had the good fortune of having worked for several outstanding managers over the years; individuals who had the experience to teach me, the temperament to lead me, the concern for me to gain my loyalty and the commitment to the mission to get the best out of me.

One that comes quickly to mind was my first trainer and crew chief in the Air Force, Bob Smitka. Growing up in New York City, I knew next to nothing about mechanics. Since most City dwellers rely on mass transportation, my lack of mechanical expertise was compounded by the fact that I had never driven a car.

My first assignment after Technical Training was to the 67th Tactical Fighter Squadron based on Okinawa. I was assigned to be Smitty's assistant on an F-105 aircraft.

Over the course of the first few months, Smitty worked me hard, taught me well and trusted me with responsibilities far beyond my experience. He forced me to drive a truck every day. In weeks, I was towing aircraft. Guiding me every step of the way, I grew by leaps and bounds in both confidence and knowledge. To this day I can still hear him saying, "Go ahead, you know how to do it."

In the end, not only had he developed a "green bean" into a qualified mechanic, he created someone who took those same values and used them when he was given responsibility for new recruits. Good management always has three bene-ficiaries: the person leading, the individuals being led and the organization - a win, win, win.

Unfortunately, we also have memories of managers who shouldn't have been managers; individuals in positions of leadership for which they have neither the experience nor ability. Do you remember your worst manager? Did your productivity improve or decline during that time? Did you learn and grow professionally? Did you feel part of something? Did good people leave the company?

Clearly, individuals lacking requisite experience and skills can inflict heavy damage on a business when placed into leadership positions. Those unfortunate souls reporting to them are particularly victimized. They're deprived of quality training, effective guidance and opportunities for advancement. Sadly, many ultimately leave the company which only adds to the costs for having an unqualified manager.

When trapped in that situation, many blame their fate on the incapable managers themselves. This is really a misguided placement of blame. The responsibility for bad managers always rests with those in the organization who have selected them. The selection of managers remains one of the most important responsibilities of every company's leaders.

One of Jack Welch's critical initiatives at General Electric was the cultivation of managers. "What we are looking for . . . are leaders . . . who can energize, excite and control rather than enervate, depress and control." [15] He placed managers into one of four separate categories:

A. Those that deliver on their commitments and share company values
B. Those that don't deliver on commitments and don't share company values
C. Those that don't deliver on commitments but share company values
D. Those that deliver on commitments but don't share company values

While he only wanted managers who both shared the company's vision and delivered on their commitments, he did give some leeway to those who subscribed to General Electric's values but hadn't yet shown the desired results. He didn't want anyone wasting time and energy trying to convert anyone who didn't subscribe to those values. [16]

Welch felt as I do; management isn't a place for individuals who place self over team. A manager is both responsible for, and responsible to, the individuals they manage. Narcissists end up short-changing both their subordinates and the company.

Managing Your Business to Its Maximum Sales Potential is a top down process. To be successful, it must be driven by the organization's leaders. Correspondingly, if a company's leadership ranks are populated by qualified, experienced people, the probability for success is greatly improved.

A review of the responsibilities the Program places on its leaders reinforces this requirement. The leaders are charged with bringing all segments of the company into a unified, cooperative group striving to the single goal of maximum sales. This requires melding such diverse disciplines as Finance, Sales, Marketing, Credit, Customer Services, Human Resources, Transportation, Management Information Services and Purchasing. Additionally, this must be done in the face of an initial resistance to change so common in business organizations.

As the Program progresses, these challenges only increase. Management must constantly reinforce the importance of the Program, monitor its progress and communicate that progress, while continually looking for ways to further improve sales performance. These Program-related responsibilities are in addition to a manager's standard responsibilities such as hiring, training, guiding and monitoring. *Managing Your Business to Its Maximum Sales*

Potential is a thorough test of any manager's complete portfolio of leadership skills.

Contrary to common belief, experience is not necessarily a function of time. A person might hold a position for years, yet not really gain experience. Experience is a product of the variety and complexity of the situations and conditions in which an individual has performed. The more familiar individuals are with different situations, particularly difficult ones, the better equipped they will be to handle those situations in the future.

Leaders must have acquired the knowledge needed to lead. They then draw on that acquired knowledge to make the most effective decisions possible. In his work, *The Effective Executive,* Peter Drucker affirms this need for superior experience (knowledge) as a criterion for leadership. "Every knowledge worker in the modern organization is an "executive" if, by virtue of his position or knowledge, he is responsible for a contribution that materially affects the capacity of the organization to perform and obtain results...he is supposed, by virtue of his knowledge, to be better equipped to make the right decision than anyone else." [17]

We live in an imperfect world. Individuals sometimes rise to positions for which they are eminently unqualified. The subjectivity of the promotion process makes it particularly vulnerable to manipulation. The elevation of unprepared individuals to leadership roles can be extremely costly to a company in terms of lost opportunities, lost productivity, lost revenues and, most devastating, lost people. Unfortunately, the bill doesn't arrive until after the damages have been inflicted.

At the height of the economic slowdown, one of our managers opened a meeting by asking, "What can I do to help increase sales?" A salesperson raised his hand and said, "Clear the decks. Eliminate all those non-selling activities like meetings and unnecessary reports."

The manager, a recent arrival from the XYZ Company, responded, "This is nothing! You should have been at XYZ. We had meetings and reports every day." The questioner then said, "XYZ is on the verge of bankruptcy. Why would we use them as our business model?"

The manager could only mumble, "Good point."

There is too much at stake for a business to be cavalier about the selection of its leaders. No business can expect to reach the goal of maximum sales, if the individuals responsible for attaining that objective are not, as Mr. Drucker says, "better equipped to make the right decision than anyone else."

Marv Levy, former coach of the Buffalo Bills defines leadership as, "the ability of getting others to get the best out of themselves." Only individuals committed to getting the best out of themselves are adequately equipped to assume that responsibility.

Regardless of the discipline, the same principle always applies; quality leadership gets desired results. Those who will lead a company to *Its Maximum Sales Potential* must have the experience, knowledge, character, integrity and commitment to excellence necessary for such a difficult, yet rewarding, journey.

Attribute #2 Questionnaire

Is the promotion process in your company fair? _____

What's the most important factor for promotion?
Explain: _____
_____

Are your current leaders the best qualified for the job?
Explain: _____
_____

Do you trust your manager? _____

Are you pleased with your professional growth? _____
Explain: _____

Do you fully understand the company's goal? _____

Does your manager personally communicate with you on
a regular basis? _____

Does he/she put the company's interests first? _____

Why were you selected to be a manager? _____
_____

Do your subordinates trust you? _____

Do you think they're pleased with how you've guided
their careers? _____

Do you meet with your subordinates individually? _____

How often? _____

Do you put the company's interests ahead of your own?
_____

Do you put the interests of your team ahead of your own?
_____

Are you the best qualified to lead your group? _____
Explain: _____
_____

What managerial quality is your weakest?
_____
_____

What's your strongest managerial quality?
_____
_____

"The toughest thing about success is that you've got to keep on being a success."

Irving Berlin
American Composer

Attribute #3

Flexible and Embraces Change

It takes courage to change. When things are going well, the tendency is to stick with what's been working. In business, however, standing pat can be a company's death knell. The blinding speed of change in today's environment combined with the solid capabilities of competitors don't allow for the luxury of sitting back and savoring past successes. In his book, *Good to Great,* Jim Collins describes this threat with his declaration, "Good is the enemy of great." [18]

Lou Gerstner of IBM sees the threat as being greatest for successful, established market leaders: "When there's little competitive threat, when high profit margins and a commanding market position are assumed . . . the company and its people lose touch with external realities because what's happening in the marketplace is essentially irrelevant to the success of the company." [19]

"The more successful an enterprise becomes, the more it wants to codify what makes it great . . . Inevitably, though, as the world changes, the rules, guidelines, and customs lose their connection to what the enterprise is all about . . . This *rigor mortis* that sets in around values and behaviors is a problem unique . . . to successful enterprises. What I think hurts the most is their inability to change highly structured . . . cultures that had been born in a different world." [20]

In business, as in life, fortunes change in a heartbeat. A friend once described the speed of change best when he said, "What we see on the news isn't news at all; it's history."

To appreciate just how quickly fortunes can change, consider several individuals profiled in the 1999 book, *Lessons from the Top: The Search for the Best Business Leaders in America.* The *Best Business Leaders* at that time the book was written included: Michael Armstrong of AT&T, Steve Case of America Online, Dennis Kozlowski of Tyco, Bernie Ebbers of WorldCom and Ken Lay of Enron. As I always say, icons today, gone tomorrow!

Not only can fortunes change quickly, the change can even hinge on a single decision. Martha Stewart's decision to save $50,000 by circumventing the system has cost her well over $500 million. The 1919 sale of Babe Ruth to the New York Yankees for $100,000 haunts the Boston Red Sox to this day.

These blunders pale, however, when compared to a decision made by William Orton, President of Western Union. In 1876, Orton rejected Alexander Graham Bell's offer to sell the patent rights for the telephone for $100,000. In doing so, he assured his place in history as, "the man who refused the most profitable invention in recorded history." [21]

As you can see, the fortunes of neither individuals nor businesses are ever assured. To thrive, companies must be prepared to change and to change quickly. They can be the catalyst for change or they can respond to changes driven by others, but they must be flexible and open to change.

I don't believe it's ever been more difficult to stay on top than it is today. The speed of technology-driven advances, regulatory issues and the evolution of the worldwide market-place make it a challenge for companies just to hold their positions.

We need only look at the speed with which online sales have invaded the once serene world of established retailers or the way litigation and regulations have limited companies like Microsoft and Phillip Morris to appreciate why companies must be on constant alert. The emergence of the world

markets has only added the many complexities of internat-
ional trade to the mix.

In such a setting, it's especially important that business
leaders always maintain a state of *confident insecurity*. They
must be confident in their abilities and decisions, yet be
vigilant to the vulnerabilities of their business.

When Jack Welch became General Electric's CEO, I was the
New York Area Manager for its Mobile Communications
Division. Most thought that changing a behemoth like GE
would take years. That clearly wasn't the case. On assuming
office, Welch immediately set his standard for performance.
He declared that any business unit not ranked #1 or #2 in its
industry would be fixed, sold or closed. He saw uncompet-
itive business units as a diversion and a drain of valuable
resources. True to his word, he proceeded to divest GE of
those businesses that failed to meet his criteria. GE was on
its way to becoming the #1 corporation in the world.

At the time, GE wasn't exactly faltering. The company had
just posted record financial results. Welch could easily have
taken the baton from his predecessor, Reg Jones, and continued with business as usual. He was uneasy though and knew
in his heart, "GE had to change before it was too late."[22]

The primary basis for his concerns was the culture that
seemed to permeate the entire organization. Everywhere he
looked, he saw the complacency borne of past successes. He
was alarmed when he heard "phrases like: 'If it ain't broke,
don't fix it' or 'Don't be a solution in search of a problem'."
[23] Fortunately for GE shareholders, Welch recognized that
success didn't mitigate the need for change.

Welch realized GE's future success would be dependent on
its ability to adapt quickly to shifting market conditions. As
he stated, "Our challenge is to make General Electric have
all the benefits of a big company and yet act with the speed,

decisiveness, and knowledge of a small company."[24]   What he was seeing at the time was a big company acting like a big company.

> **"All organizations do change when put under sufficient pressure. This pressure must be either external to the organization or the result of very strong leadership."**
>
> **Bruce Henderson**
> CEO, Boston Consulting Group

Dell, Inc. is another classic example of a corporation leading by constant change. Since its creation in 1984, Michael Dell has been one of the most innovative, flexible and successful executives in the history of American business. In fact, for anyone truly wanting to learn the principles of effective management, Dell's autobiography, "Direct from Dell" is required reading.

A cunning visionary, he has consistently capitalized on opportunities in an industry filled with capable competitors and cost-conscious, savvy customers. In this environment, Dell has guided his company to the top of the industry by instilling flexibility and speed throughout the organization. Technology analyst, Ashok Kumar describes it this way, "His (Dell's) competitors are like sumo wrestlers. Dell is more like a kick boxer." [25]

Throughout his career, Dell has consistently exhibited that rare combination of seeing opportunities before others and having the courage to act on them. He saw the void in product support that plagued the early personal computer industry. To Dell, that weakness spelled opportunity. He quickly became the first manufacturer to sell made-to-order PCs directly to the customer. Eliminating the middleman afforded him substantial pricing advantages over competitors. He soon became the first PC manufacturer to offer next-day, on-site technical support. To allay customer fears about buying a computer sight unseen, he introduced the Dell thirty day money-back guarantee. All of his success is founded on one simple principle: there's a better way to provide personal computers to the public. He was the agent for change in the PC industry.

As with any innovator, there were failures along the way. He responded to such setbacks with the same flexibility and speed that have been hallmarks of his successes. When he attempted to use third party distributors to gain entry into the retail market, he quickly recognized he was going away from his strengths and returned to his more effective direct model.

Recognizing the promise of the internet, he introduced *www.dell.com* in 1994. Shortly thereafter, he introduced online configuration to the web site allowing customers to design units to their exact specifications. The results have been, and continue to be, nothing short of startling.

Dell, Inc. is still evolving to this day. Manufacturing plants are open in Europe and Asia and the product line has been expanded to include servers, notebooks, PDA's and printers. Only recently, Dell entered the $95 billion consumer electronics industry with a portable digital music player, an online music store and a flat panel television. I'm sure companies involved in that business were just elated to hear that!

Nothing validates the power of flexibility and openness to change more than success. Between 1991 and 1997, General Electric's revenues quadrupled, and its earnings rose almost 500%, while its workforce was reduced by 37%. [26]

Dell's results have been equally amazing. With splits, 100 shares of Dell purchased in January 1992 grew into 9,600 shares in March of 1999. Not resting on its laurels, Dell has assumed the position of #1 producer of personal computers in the world.

Could these results have been realized if the leaders of either of these companies chose to defy the gods of change and stuck with the *status quo*? The answer is obvious.

The *Managing Your Business to Its Maximum Sales Potential* Program is a blueprint for change. It's clearly not intended for businesses that are satisfied with their current performance. Its potential will be readily apparent, however, to any business leader who recognizes the fragility of success and understands, "The future is made in the present." [27]

Attribute #3 Questionnaire

Is your company more apt to initiate or react to industry changes?_____
Give examples:_____

Is there a formal process in place for gathering information on competitors? _____

If no, how are competitive activities tracked?
_____

Who oversees this process?
_____

How are these findings communicated to the CEO and other executives? _____
_____

What's the greatest threat to the company today?
_____

Could the internal operations be improved? _____
How? _____
_____

Does a program exist for evaluating internal processes?
_____ **Explain:** _____

Is there a suggestion program in place? _____
Explain: _____

If not, how do people communicate their ideas?
_____

How quickly are suggestions reviewed and acted on?

_____

Does management encourage suggestions?

_____

Do people in your department make many suggestions?
_____

Why? _____

Do you make many suggestions? _____

What was your last suggestion? _____

_____

Was it acted on? _____
Explain: _____

_____

Is the company resistant to making changes? _____

_____

_____

What are its greatest impediments to change?

_____

_____

"Too much energy is being used up in corporate in-fighting. The corporation ought to be devoting it energies to making the finest cars in the world, and not get tied up in Machiavellian intrigues."

H. Ross Perot
on the Problems at General Motors

Attribute #4

Minimal Internal Politics

We've all sensed it, been affected by it and even adjusted our behavior in response to it. And, we have all worked with people who specialized in it.

The "it" I'm referring to is office politics.

What exactly is office politics? I define it as the cultural force within business organizations by which activities are governed more by how they'll be perceived than what they'll produce. Although its influence varies by company, politics always extracts a price.

It's like driving a car while using a cell phone and looking for change in your wallet. The more the distractions, the greater the odds you're going to crash. Politics has the same effect on businesses. When employees become preoccupied with internal intrigues, their attention to revenue-generating activities are diminished.

In every organization, there's a constant give and take between politics and productivity. When the balance tips in the favor of one, it does so at the expense of the other.

Politics is the single most destructive force in any company – the ultimate inefficiency. It's the cholesterol of the business organization. Stealthily, it clogs its arteries, undermines the effective use of its resources and saps the strength it needs to compete. Over time, the ravages of the disease progress to the point that extreme measures must be taken or the patient (the business) will expire.

> **People busy covering their rears are wasting energy and time that ought to be devoted to challenging competitors.**
>
> **Daniel Greenberg**
> Chairman, Electro Rent Corp.

Attaining maximum sales requires the full commitment of all of an organization's resources. When politics enters the mix, it slows productivity, engenders distrust and diverts attention away from the organization's sales and earnings goal. For all of these reasons, discouraging politics and behaviors that foster politics is Attribute #4 of the *Maximum Sales Potential* Program.

Arguably, the greatest threat that politics poses to a business is the role it plays in the promotion process. It allows individuals to rise to leadership positions for reasons other than their abilities, experience and work quality. Moving from a merit-based promotion system controlled by accomplishment and ability to one dominated by the superficiality of politics weakens any organization.

> **"You can't get you finger on the problem if you've got it to the wind."**
>
> **Congressman Dick Armey**
> *Armey's Axioms*

Political promotions can easily set off a long-term cycle of ineffective management. Just as we all tend to gravitate to like-thinking individuals, politically-motivated individuals, when promoted, also surround themselves with individuals who share their views. Once entrenched, these individuals influence and control most of the activities throughout the company.

Politically-based promotions are a double edged sword; less qualified individuals assume positions of leadership, while more qualified candidates are denied advancement. Soon, the more qualified ones leave the company (frequently going to competitors), while the performance of the company is left in the hands of those less qualified. Unfortunately, the skills and experience needed for maximum performance are also departing with the more qualified employees.

I've been told many times that politics can never be eliminated from a business. I couldn't disagree more.

My research reveals I'm in very good company. In his first meeting with IBM's Corporate Management Board, the corporation's top fifty executives, Lou Gerstner clearly saw the dangers that internal politics and a bloated hierarchy posed to his mission of turning around this once great company. He stunned the attendees when he proclaimed one of his basic philosophies, "I look for people who work to solve problems and help colleagues. I sack politicians. . . Hierarchy means very little to me . . .Reduce committees and meetings to a minimum. No committee decision making." [28]

Like all cultural factors within an organization, politics is a top-down phenomenon. Employees instinctively behave in ways they believe will be viewed favorably by the executives and managers. It then follows that the actions, reactions, directives, decisions and styles of these same executives and managers establish the degree to which politics will be accepted within the company. In fact, the day leadership wants to eliminate politics from a company is the day it will literally disappear. Leadership's use of this influence to minimize politics is critical for any company striving to reach its *Maximum Sales Potential*.

I've seen so many instances throughout my career when executives and managers have ordained political behaviors as acceptable. Some were career politicians themselves, however, most just failed to realize how their behaviors were being interpreted by others. Regardless of the reason, the end result was the same – lower productivity.

If a company hopes to eliminate politics, its leaders must be sure the messages they're sending aren't perceived as an endorsement of political behavior. Here are some of the common actions that might be misinterpreted by employees throughout the organization:

- Not challenging individuals who assign blame to others. John Peers, President of Logical Machine Company, calls this the, "It's not whether you win or lose, but how you place the blame" strategy.[29] The failure to challenge this behavior is seen as being accepting it. Before long, placing blame on others becomes a standard defense for individual performance issues in the future.

- Recommending politically-motivated individuals for advancement. This is interpreted by others as a clear statement by management that political status is more important than actual performance for growing in the company. Apolitical employees will now invest time focusing on how they're being perceived, as opposed to what they're producing. Company performance can only be hurt by this scenario.

- Rewarding political behavior is seen as endorsing it. We've all worked with individuals who have spent more time trying to impress the boss than actually doing their jobs. When these individuals enjoy preferential treatment, others in the department feel slighted. Inevitably, this leads to dissension in the ranks and a corresponding decline in productivity. Loyalty to management is also compromised.

- Most people work within the current paradigm, while a smaller percentage of others tend to challenge current methods. If the latter group is met with criticism, management has declared its preference for individuals who don't challenge the *status quo*. Unfortunately, those individuals avoid the risks inherent to change that are so critical to the survival of every business. Challenging current methods is a sign of a healthy business and those who offer up those challenges are vital to its growth. Michael Dell puts it this way, "To encourage people to innovate more, you have to make it safe for them to fail." [30]

- We've all received e-mails from people who have also copied the entire world. More often than not, politics is the sender's primary motivation. The way management responds will indicate whether or not such correspondence is acceptable. If management wishes to put an end to this type of correspondence, the ranking recipient of the e-mail need only respond to the sender asking why multiple individuals were copied. All individuals receiving the original e-mail should be copied on this response to ensure the disapproval is clearly communicated for all to see.

> **"A memorandum is written not to inform the reader but to protect the writer."**
> **Dean Acheson**
> U.S. Secretary of State

- Refusal by a manager to make decisions or to take action for fear of personal risk is politics by example. Overt political sensitivity by a leader causes others to act and think similarly. Such individuals usually try to disguise their true intentions behind contrivances like needing more information or suggesting that a meeting or committee be convened to review the issue. Such inaction is actually a decision to place personal interests over those of the company – politics over productivity.

- Showing preferential treatment to select individuals is a common way managers endorse politics. I knew a sales manager who only invited several favored members of his team and their spouses to a Saturday evening dinner. Amazingly, he was oblivious to how the other members would react to this obvious slight. Not surprisingly, his team ended the year 25% under target.

These are just some of the ways managers can unwittingly promote office politics. In light of the damage it can inflict on productivity, it's critically important that every leader recognize their influence throughout the organization and take steps to ensure the role of politics is limited.

There is one final area where leaders in a business must be particularly alert. That's the role politics can play in the dealings between departments.

In business organizations, departments normally have the authority to mandate policies and procedures for their particular areas of responsibility. Even in ideal environments, these can be breeding grounds for inefficiencies. In very political environments, however, this authority can easily be misused for departmental or individual purposes. When that's the case, waste is bound to result.

Unnecessary procedures or policies might be mandated for any of the following reasons:

- To protect the interests of a particular department
- To lessen a department's workload by causing delays
- To exert control over other departments or managers
- To gain exposure for the department or its managers

When based on sound business principles, policies and procedures are vital to the effective operation of a business. When created for political purposes, however, they exact a huge toll in wasted time, distrust and misplaced energies.

The negative aspects of politics within a business should be obvious. Its costs in resources, energy, focus, morale and turnover can be devastating. In fact, no company in which politics plays a major role in its activities, its decision-making or its selection of leaders has any chance of ever reaching its full sales potential.

Looking back over the years, I've come to the realization that politics was only a minor force in the most productive companies with which I've been associated. Those that struggled for results were always consumed by political intrigue and internal distrust.

It doesn't have to be that way. Starting with the CEO, the executives and managers choose the degree of influence politics will have in their company.

In business, politics is just a euphemism for self-interest. Management is faced with the choice of whether it wants personal self-interest or the interests of the organization to dominate the attitudes and behavior of the employees. Only when it's the latter is their organization positioned to reach its *Maximum Sales Potential.*

President Ronald Reagan was aware of the limitations that politics imposes on performance. Prominently displayed on his desk was a sign with the message, "It's a wonder how much can get done when no one is concerned with who gets the credit."

Attribute #4 Questionnaire

From 1 - 10 (10 the highest), how much of a factor is politics in your company? _____

On the same scale, to what degree does politics govern your behavior? _____

Are promotions based on merit? _____

If not, what are they based on? _____
_____

What was the basis for your most recent promotion?
Explain: _____
_____

How much of your workday is spent doing unnecessary activities? _____ %

Do the people and departments in your company work cooperatively? _____ Explain: _____
_____

Which people are the most difficult to work with?
_____
Why: _____
_____

Do you trust your co-workers? _____

Your manager? _____

Your CEO? _____

If no to any one, explain: _____

_____

Are you more concerned with what your work produces or how it's perceived? Explain: _____

_____

Does that apply to most people in your company? Explain: _____

If all unnecessary demands were removed, would your productivity increase? _____

Name some of the unproductive demands.

_____

_____

Which are the most taxing?

_____

_____

_____

If they're hurting productivity, why do you think they exist in the first place? Explain: _____

_____

Should you be promoted? _____

Do you think you will be? _____

Why? _____

_____

"One hand cannot applaud alone"

Arabian Proverb

Attribute #5

Sales-Friendly Culture

The dominant factor in determining the way an organization operates is its culture. It dictates the standards for behavior, priorities, how individuals and departments interact and all other variables within a business.

Like so many other internal factors, an organization's culture is built from the top down. The preferences and expectations that comprise a company's culture are the preferences and expectations of its leaders. In a business organization, the president, CEO, and other senior executives establish the culture.

In their book, Every Business is a Growth Business, Ram Charan and Noel Tichy describe the evolutionary process of a company's culture this way. "The code (culture) originates with the organization's leaders – their thinking and behaviors send signals and cues that set the pattern for everyone else. In time, these become the organization's genetic code. And this code is all-pervasive. . .The signals it sends, influence how people think and behave in all areas of their working lives . . . In the end, they determine whether the corporation succeeds or fails." [31]

Lou Gerstner also understood the importance culture played in his turnaround efforts at IBM. "I came to see . . . that culture isn't just one aspect of the game – it is the game. In the end, an organization is nothing more than the collective capacity of its people to create value. Vision, strategy, marketing, financial management – any management system can set you on the right path . . .But no enterprise . . . will succeed over the long haul if those elements aren't part of its DNA." [32]

To attain its *Maximum Sales Potential*, a company must have a culture that supports that objective – a sales culture. Since only the leaders have the authority and influence to create such a culture, it's their responsibility then to define, adopt, communicate and reinforce an environment in which sales performance dominates all activities.

A sales-friendly culture is one that includes each of the following characteristics:

- Maximum sales is the company's goal
- Sales performance is the responsibility of all employees
- All employees see themselves as salespeople
- The impact on sales performance is a key consideration in all decision-making
- The Sales Department is viewed favorably throughout the organization
- All employees must share financially in the company's sales growth

Let's look at each of these individually:

Maximum sales is the company's goal:
This is Attribute #1. Establishing sales as the company's goal is the first step in the process of leading a company to its *Maximum Sales Potential*.

Sales performance is the responsibility of all employees:
This is the sign of a committed, sales-friendly company. All too often, sales performance is viewed throughout a company as the exclusive responsibility of the Sales Department. To reach its *Maximum Sales Potential,* all employees must recognize their role in the success or failure of their company's sales performance. This facilitates universal cooperation and commitment to the attainment of that goal.

All employees see themselves as salespeople:

This may be the most important cultural trait of all. Most people in a business think only the individual who deals directly with the customer is the salesperson..

In a sales-friendly culture, <u>every person or thing that directly or indirectly influences the sale is a salesperson</u>. By this definition, the receptionist and the driver who delivers the order are both salespeople. Inanimate objects should also be viewed as salespeople. For instance, I view a company's voicemail system as one of its salespeople. If you don't believe me, have your system lead customers on a circular journey of prompts and see if sales don't decline. Even a company invoice is a salesperson since a confusing bill will drive away customers as quickly as a bad product or service.

It's amazing how few individuals in a business see themselves as salespeople. Most are oblivious to the importance their day-to-day actions play in determining the sales success of their company. We see examples of this every day.

The clerk in the store who, when asked if they have a certain style dress in your size, gives you that glassy-eyed, vacuous, I-couldn't-care-less stare, and mumbles, "Only what's on the rack." The result is a lost sale and, quite probably, a lost customer.

You go to a local restaurant. The meal is delicious, the bread has an aroma to die for and the wine is the finest vintage. The service, however, leaves much to be desired. Even the exceptional quality of the fare won't bring you back. If you told the waiter he was hurting restaurant sales, he'd probably respond, "I'm not a salesman, I'm a waiter."

Customers base their buying decisions in a large part on the quality of service they receive, in other words, how they're treated. Professor Francis Petit, Assistant Dean of Fordham

81

University's Graduate School of Business, calls this "managing all of the experiences in the customer interface process."

Clearly, a company with a culture in which everyone is a salesperson has a far better chance of positively managing those experiences than one that doesn't.

The impact on sales performance is a key consideration in all decision making:

Most inefficiencies are caused by the failure of decision-makers to consider all the possible ramifications of their decisions. This oversight leads to redundancies, unnecessary activities and other drains on company resources.

The departmental structure in most businesses also contributes to this problem. Since performances under this structure are measured strictly on the basis of the results realized by each individual department, parochial decision-making is to be expected.

To negate this tendency, companies must adopt a holistic approach to decision-making. This requires that consideration be given to the impact each decision will have on every segment of a business (its *impact field*). In the *Maximum Sales Potential* Program, particular attention must be paid to the impact decisions will have on sales performance.

Applying a holistic approach to all decisions is so crucial to the sales success of a business, it's Attribute #8 of the Program.

The Sales Department is viewed favorably throughout the organization:

For reasons I've never fully understood, the Sales Department in many companies is often seen as the problem child by other departments. This often gives rise to a practice I call *Sales Bashing* in which Sales is blamed for any organizational shortcoming and its efforts are impeded with impunity by other departments.

As with all things cultural, *Sales Bashing* is a reflection of management's attitude. Through their words and actions, leadership sets the tone for how Sales is viewed. Members of the organization follow their cue. The following is an example of how one manager led the charge:

Having missed their sales target, the General Manager sent a terse voicemail to all employees voicing his displeasure and stating he was taking the following corrective action: "Effective immediately, Friday casual dress privileges are suspended for all members of the SALES DEPARTMENT. The privileges will be reinstated once our sales performance improves."

In just one voicemail, he violated two core principles of *Managing Your Business to Its Maximum Sales Potential*. He blamed the sales shortfall exclusively on the Sales Department and he absolved all other segments of the organization of any responsibility for the company's sales performance.

Not surprisingly, sales performance didn't improve.

Because his view of Sales had already been embedded, the rest of the organization willingly followed his lead. Sales was being continually burdened with non-selling activities and the lack of internal cooperation was a constant problem. To no one's surprise, sales growth was virtually nonexistent.

All employees must share financially in the company's sales growth:

This is the most overlooked of the six characteristics of a sales-friendly culture. Companies consistently fail to utilize this most effective tool.

Several years ago, I called our Customer Services to find out the status of an order. When the representative answered, I casually asked, "How are things going?" "Terrible," he barked, "Damn phones haven't stopped ringing all day!"

As a salesperson, this was great news. Apparently not everyone shared my view. As I thought about it, however, I realized that the only reward this fellow, and many like him, received for my sales successes was more work. No wonder he wasn't doing cartwheels!

The compensation structure in most companies has historically been salary plus benefits. There have been few innovations over the years. Each year, increases of between 1% and 3% are accompanied by a promise of even greater riches next year. Other than executives, sales reps and sales managers, no one in most companies shares financially in its sales growth.

It's foolhardy to think today's workers will make the commitment necessary for maximum performance without some financial considerations. The time has come for companies to adopt pro-growth compensation strategies.

No company can logically expect to reach maximum sales without economic incentives for all employees. Economic Value Added (EVA) and other attempts at innovation indicate that management recognizes the need for some type of financial mechanism as a catalyst for growth. To date, however, these have been woefully inadequate in both dollars and payout frequency.

If a company wants maximum sales growth, it will have to pay for it. Any business with the courage to develop a formula that effectively does that will be rewarded with sales and earnings growth not otherwise attainable. Under this Program, adopting a growth-oriented approach to compensation is of such importance that it has been adopted as Attribute #11.

Unfortunately, employees in most companies see sales as an abstract — some distant event for which they have no responsibility, can make little impact and receive no financial reward. This sense of detachment is cultural and can only be changed from the top down.

To reach its full sales potential, a company's culture must be one in which the entire organization is totally committed to reaching that goal. Working in an environment governed by a sales-friendly culture makes that goal a far more realistic probability. If such a culture is to be a reality, it is up to the company's leaders to establish it.

SALES RESPONSIBILITIES
IN A SALES-FRIENDLY CULTURE

Attribute #5 Questionnaire

Are you responsible for company sales performance?
_____ **Explain:** _____
_____

What were your company's total sales last month?
$_____

Was that an increase or decrease from the prior month?
_____

How is Sales viewed within your company?
Favorably   _____   **Necessary Evil**   _____
Inconvenience   _____   **Unfavorably**   _____
Explain: _____
_____

Do your daily activities affect sales performance? _____
Explain: _____
_____

Do you receive compensation for sales growth? _____

Does that affect the way you do your job? _____
Explain: _____

If you lost money when sales were lower, would it affect your job performance? _____
Explain: _____

Have your ever spent a day with a salesperson? _____

How often do you interact with customers? _____

What's the most difficult task of a salesperson?

_____

If you were offered a position in Sales, would you take it?
_____ **Explain why:** _____

_____

Why do you think the company's sales aren't higher?

_____

_____

**What changes to the internal organization would you
make to increase sales?** _____

_____

_____

If sales go down, would you be worried for your job?
_____ **Explain:** _____

_____

In business, the difference between success and failure is always customers. Never let them forget that!

The Author

Attribute #6

<u>Enjoyable Customer Experience</u>

Most of us don't go where we feel we're not wanted. This is certainly true of customers. Another major factor in the sales performance equation is how enjoyable a company makes it for customers to do business with them. The quality of the product or service is only one part of the formula. Features such as promptness, courtesy, flexibility, attention to detail, enthusiasm, accessibility and responsiveness are also critical factors in determining sales performance.

Businesses control much of their own success. They can't really influence the external factors, but they have direct control over the internal ones. A company's operational efficiency, the attitude of its workers, the support of its product or service and its culture are all under its direct control.

Who within an organization controls these factors? Quite simply, its leaders do. The executives and managers dictate the quality of every facet of their company's service.

The buying experience is driven by the culture of the business. Since culture is a top down phenomenon, once again, it is reflection of the CEO and the other leaders in the organization. Therefore, if a company provides poor service, its executives and managers *have chosen* to provide poor service. Conversely, good service is the product of capable, concerned and committed leadership.

My first sales manager, Dave Polley, always stressed, "Just keep crossing the bridge." Dave felt that everyone knows how they like to be treated when they're the buyer. So, he concluded, when you're the seller, you need only cross over that mental bridge from buyer to seller and provide the same quality of service you look for when you're the buyer.

The buying experience doesn't have to be euphoric. It must, however, be respectful of the time, preferences and desires of the buyer. Arrogant proclamations like the old, "When E.F. Hutton talks, people listen," represent an inverted view of reality. Had their philosophy been, "When people talk, E.F. Hutton listens," perhaps they'd still be in business.

Between downsizing, controlling expenses and other constraints, poor service has become commonplace. The clerk who doesn't say thank you, the extended wait on the phone, having to jump through hoops to return an item, indifferent customer services representatives; the list of affronts to the customer goes on and on. Unfortunately, we can all relate to poor service.

CompUSA is a classic example. I've never been inside a CompUSA store that didn't have an army of workers, easily identifiable in the bright red shirts, walking around the store. I have also never been in a CompUSA that didn't have a line at the register. They open and close registers according to some secret logarithmic formula that ensures there's always a line. It's amazing to watch. If there's one customer waiting to check out, no registers are open. If there are two customers, one register is open. Three customers still result in only one register because if they opened a second register there'd be no line at one of them! With the arrival of a fourth customer, register #2 is finally opened There MUST be a line!

Grand Union, a corporate icon for generations of American families, is an example of a business killed by its own hand. Based on my own experiences, I would have been surprised had they not recently been forced to declare bankruptcy.

Food Town, the only supermarket in my town, had closed. A&P purchased the location but delayed opening for three months for renovations. People were now forced to use the next closest supermarket, Grand Union. For three months, Grand Union was given the unique opportunity to convert their competitor's customers by merely showing their appreciation in the form of good service. Their indifference bordered on disdain. No additional help was hired and the lines only got longer. You stood a better chance of seeing the manager on the side of a milk carton than mixing with the customers.

When A&P opened, the customers, not surprisingly, voted with their feet. How could a once great franchise with a loyal following commit suicide? Quite simply, they made the buying experience neither enjoyable nor convenient.

More often than not, it's the little things that differentiate quality from poor service. I recently purchased a tennis bracelet for my wife at an upscale department store. After the clerk processed my credit card, she began wrapping the bracelet in tissue paper. When I asked for a box, she said, "We're all out of boxes." I handed back my card and said, "Issue a credit." She looked incredulous as she processed my credit. I bought the bracelet from a competitor who had boxes.

Contrast that with the quality of service you receive at a retail institution like Tiffany's. Every counter is staffed with sales professionals who are knowledgeable and helpful. Returns are directed to a separate area where you sit with another professional to process the paperwork. Questions are clearly designed to gain information needed to improve service in the future. Painless, prompt, and pleasurable – you'll be back. You see, at Tiffany's everyone is a salesperson.

Because it's the source for most purchases, the retail world provides some of the most familiar examples of poor buying experiences. Retail, however, hasn't cornered the market on poor service. Big and small, private and public, there's no shortage of companies that make the buying experience unnecessarily difficult.

I recently bought the downloadable version of a popular anti-virus program. As so often happens, there were minor compatibility issues with the installation, so I called the company for advice. For over five minutes I listened to a message telling me how pleased they were to have me as a customer and that I could get an immediate support on their 900 line for $2.95/ minute. When a representative finally did pick up, she said she couldn't help and referred me to the pay-for-service line. I presented her with another alternative, "Better than that, just issue a credit to my account. Your competitor can help me."

When I got off the phone, I wondered, "Where was this person's manager?" Then it dawned on me; probably busy processing credits.

A questionable commitment to product support is evident in most companies where the customer services representatives refuse to give their names. When you call for product support, you must give your full name and other personal information, yet when you ask the representatives for their full name, they say, "We're not allowed to give our names for security reasons." Huh? Or they say, "Just ask for John." Here's a company with 10,000 employees and when I call tomorrow and ask for John, they'll undoubtedly say, "What's his last name? We have many John's." I'll bet you do.

It's not that companies don't know how to provide good service. Look at the speed of the response when calling to make a purchase? Compare that to the delays you must endure when calling for product support.

How can the leadership of any business allow this to happen? Product support and courtesy are two of the most critical factors that engender loyalty. No businesses should ever forget it's far easier to serve your present customer than it is to find a new one.

It is impossible to effectively run a business if you're not aware of what your customers want and how they're being treated. The CEOs of any company can get a good idea of the quality of service the customers are receiving merely by anonymously calling their own support and sales lines. If they then contacted the managers of those departments to share their findings, the quality of service to the customers would improve immediately.

There was a time in the not too distant past when the president, CEO or some other executive would contact customers directly to get a sense of their key concerns. When was the last time any president or CEO called you for feedback? For that matter, when was the last time one called you just to say thank you?

Today, most executives do just the opposite. They insulate themselves from customers, thereby, denying themselves invaluable, unfiltered information so vital for effectively guiding their companies. In most companies, a bureaucratic moat is built around its leaders to ensure no one, particularly customers, can gain access to them.

Speaking directly to customers should be a standard daily practice for every executive in a company. Those that adopt this practice will find that the fifteen minutes they spend doing this each day will save time, money and, most importantly, customers.

By failing to communicate directly with customers on a regular basis, leaders place their business at risk. For all they know, they might be presiding over a Potemkin village in which information they receive has been filtered to conceal the realities of customer dissatisfaction and a dwindling customer base.

> **In preparation for a visit to his district by the Queen, Catherine the Great, Gregori Potemkin, a Russian general and statesman erected rows of elaborate cardboard houses along the route the Queen was to travel. In creating the facade of prosperity, Potemkin successfully hid the realities of poverty and unrest from the Queen.**

No company should ever underestimate the long-term memory of customers. The buying experience it provides is emblazoned in their minds. If they've been treated with considerate service at a fair price, customers will reward a company with their future business. On the other hand, they'll drop those that are indifferent to their wants and feelings more quickly than you can say, "Chapter 11."

Tip O'Neil, former Speaker of the House, shared an experience that everyone in business should remember. After being defeated in his first bid for public office, O'Neil's next door neighbor, an elderly Irish woman who had known him since birth, told him she didn't vote for him. Disappointed and confused, he asked why. "Because you never asked," she replied. After that, O'Neil never forgot that all politics is local. Perhaps all business is, too.

Maximum sales performance will never be attained by any company that doesn't consistently show its appreciation to its customers. Cute jingles and quaint messages are fluff. The universal language of customer appreciation is good products and services, consideration, respect and a fair price: the same things we expect when we're the buyer.

After all these years, I guess Dave had it right. To reach its maximum sales potential, a company must make sure that every employee keeps "crossing that bridge."

Attribute #6 Questionnaire

Is your company easy to do business with? _____
Explain: _____

Is the customer's buying experience emphasized by management? _____
How? _____

How does your company communicate with customers?
_____

Does the CEO communicate regularly with customers?
Explain: _____

When I call for service, how long do I wait before I speak to a person? _____

When I call to place an order, how long do I wait? _____

How do Customer Service reps identify themselves?
Full Name _____   **First Name Only** _____
Rep # _____   **Other** _____

Do both sales and service use the same phone #? _____

How does the company show appreciation to customers?
Explain: _____
_____

How do your competitors show their appreciation?
Explain: _____
_____

Does the company treat its customers the way you like to
be treated when you buy? _____
Explain: _____

_____

How would you improve the way customers are treated?

_____

_____

_____

Are sales growing for the company? _____

What's the percentage growth over last year? _____

What percentage of your current customers are new?
_____%

What's the main reason customers don't return to your
company? _____

_____

"In the final analysis, the one quality that all successful people have is the ability to take on responsibility."

Michael Korda

Attribute #7

Management is Responsible for Sales

In every business, the CEO, executives and managers are the individuals most responsible for its sales performance. After all, they're the ones who approve the strategies, oversee the budgets and dictate the company's policies, aren't they?

This contradicts the commonly held misperception that holds the Sales Department exclusively responsible for the sales success or failure of the company. In this section, we will identify management's direct control over all of the factors that determine sales performance. In doing so, we will be placing responsibility for sales performance squarely on the shoulders of the company's leaders. This is a most important step in the Program for before any business can hope to reach its maximum sales potential, its leaders must fully understand that their decisions, more than any other internal factor, determine sales performance.

This is not intended to assign blame. In identifying exactly who controls those factors that determine sales performance, we have identified who must initiate the actions needed to lead a business to its maximum sales potential.

A manager asked me how I had failed to successfully complete a sale we had been working on. I told him the prospect was offered more attractive prices from a competitor. He then asked why I had proposed such high prices. I reminded him it was he who had set our pricing.

He really meant to ask how <u>we</u> had lost the sale.

There are a number of warning signs that indicate when leadership doesn't recognize its role in the company's sales performance. Most obvious is when it's overseeing a culture that is unfriendly to Sales.

As covered in Attribute #5, the culture in a company is determined by its leaders. When that culture is adversarial to the needs of Sales, those leaders have failed in their responsibility.

Other signs include making demands that divert substantial amounts of time to non-selling activities, not investing in sales-growth initiatives such as lead generation programs or adopting a rigid stance on such customer-sensitive issues as credit limits, collections, returns or refunds. The most telling indicator, however, is when leadership turns a deaf ear to the needs and concerns of either the Sales organization or the customers.

When management assigns responsibility for sales performance to the Sales Department, others in the organization are quick to follow their lead. This can set a very dangerous precedent within a business. Attitudes towards Sales tend to harden, sales-related processes are treated with indifference and customers are viewed as an inconvenience.

Management literally controls every one of the factors that determine sales performance. On first blush, this might appear to be an overestimation of managerial influence. On closer examination, however, the link becomes obvious.

The following chart identifies some common sales-related problems along with some of the more probable causes for each. On the left, the problems are listed, while the right hand column cites potential causes for each. As you will see, management decisions determine each potential cause.

PROBLEM	POTENTIAL CAUSES
Salespeople leave after their first year	Poor hiring practices Unfair territory assignments Nepotism and politics Too many salespeople Insufficient administrative support Compensation isn't competitive No opportunities for career growth Lack of effective training
Sales always slow in the 4th quarter	Poorly structured or "capped" commission plan Unrealistic quotas Diminished expectations
High turnover in Sales	Compensation isn't competitive No opportunities for career growth Lack of adequate sales support No lead generation programs Incapable management Internal politics Excessive demands on selling time
Excessive customer churn	Customers don't feel appreciated Inconsistent services or support Uncompetitive pricing Difficult buying experience Inflexible collection procedures Impolite support or sales staff Lack of new value-added services Difficult to understand invoicing Poor communication with customers Organizational inflexibility Commitments not honored
Not enough new accounts	No financial incentives for growth Targeting incorrect markets Insufficient or ineffective advertising Ineffective marketing materials No lead generation support Excessive new account procedures Inflexible credit policies/procedures Too many non-selling demands Lack of innovation

Let's look at the first problem: salespeople are leaving the company after one year. The potential causes cited include: poor hiring practices, unfair territory assignments, nepotism and politics, overstaffing, insufficient support, below-market compensation, limited opportunities for growth and lack of training. Either through its control over the allocation of resources, the establishment of sales strategies, approval of policies or defining the organization's culture, management directly controls each these factors.

Each is the result of some decision made by management. Since management controls the factors causing these problems, it's logical to conclude that only they have the influence and authority needed to change them.

The same linkage applies to any of the problems on the list. Management's control might be budgetary, cultural or strategic, but its role as the final arbiter for each of the potential causes is undeniable.

This will almost certainly be seen as revolutionary in most companies. *Managing Your Business to Its Maximum Sales Potential,* however, is based on questioning current methods and thinking. By identifying management's control over sales performance, we've accomplished two very important things:

- We've identified who in the organization must be the catalysts for change

- We've refuted the belief that the Sales Department holds exclusive responsibility for company sales performance. This is a critically important step towards gaining the full participation and cooperation of every employee needed to bring the company to its full sales potential.

Outstanding sales performance is always the result of the guidance provided by a company's leadership. Conversely, inferior sales performance is always the product of their ineffective decisions or directives.

For a business to reach its full sales potential, its executives and managers must recognize their individual and collective responsibility for achieving that objective. Every aspect of a business' success, particularly its sales performance, is dependent on the quality of its leader's decisions. Until management recognizes and accepts this responsibility, companies will continue to waste valuable time and resources in a fruitless search for sales excellence.

Attribute #7 Questionnaire

Who's responsible for sales in your company? _____
_____

What's your role in the company's sales performance?
Explain: _____
_____

On a scale of 1 – 10 (10 the highest), how important do
you feel sales is to the success of the company? _____

Would other managers rate it similarly? _____
Explain: _____

How do your decisions impact sales performance?
_____
_____

Is this a consideration in your decision-making? _____
Explain: _____
_____

On a scale of 1 – 10 (10 the highest), how does the CEO
rate the importance of sales performance? _____

How does the CEO view the role of the Sales Department?
Critically Important _____
Important _____
Fairly Important _____
Somewhat Important _____

How do managers view the role of the Sales Department?
Critically Important _____
Important _____
Fairly Important _____
Somewhat Important _____

How do other employees view the role of the Sales?
Critically Important _____
Important _____
Fairly Important _____
Somewhat Important _____

When sales performance is below expectations, what actions are taken internally?
Explain: _____

_____

Does everyone look first to the Sales Department? _____
Explain: _____
Why? _____

Does the entire organization join in the effort to improve sales? _____
Explain: _____

_____

"A business organization is like the human body. When just one part gets infected, the whole body gets a fever."

The Author

Attribute #8

Decisions are Made Holistically

No decision is ever an isolated event.

Decisions are like stones tossed into a tranquil pond. The splash at the point of impact is followed by a series of ripples. The ripples continue long after the impact point has disappeared.

Business decisions have the same effect. The interrelationship between the segments of a business organization virtually assures that every decision will affect other segments in some way. In the *Maximum Sales Potential* Program, this is known as a decision's impact field.

To appreciate just how far-reaching these secondary effects can be, let's look at the impact field resulting from the change in a company's return policy from 30 to 20 days. This relatively minor change in policy will probably trigger the following actions within the organization:

- The revised policy must be announced to all departments.
- The policy must be announced to all customers
- Customer Services will require extra time to explain the change to customers.
- The Sales Department must also explain the change to resistant customers.
- Exceptions must be addressed for customers with valid reasons for having missed the deadline.
- A/R must manually apply credits for these exceptions.
- All promotional materials and signage (brochures, cash receipts etc.) showing the former policy must be updated.
- All contracts must be reviewed to ensure the new policy doesn't violate previous agreements with customers.

- Receivables must be monitored as customers withhold payments pending application of credits.

Other considerations might include the tracking of inventory and potential competitive disadvantages resulting from the modification. Clearly, the change in policy wasn't a simple or isolated event.

Unfortunately, all the possible effects are rarely considered before decisions are made. As shown above, the *impact field* for even the most basic decision is far wider than would normally have been anticipated.

We had a Credit manager who instituted a policy of notifying all past due customers that their accounts would be forwarded to an outside collection agency, if payment wasn't received immediately. He was sure this would put an end to late payments. It nearly put an end to all payments!

He had failed to consider the history of the customers being notified. Some of the company's most loyal customers also received notifications.

As quickly as you can say, "We should have thought this through," irate customers were burning up the lines. We spent the next few weeks trying to undo the damage caused by this person's failure to consider all the possible consequences of his decision.

As stated previously, the organizational structure of most businesses along with the way individual performances are measured don't promote panoramic evaluations when making decisions. Since everyone's status, compensation and job security is tied exclusively to the performance of their department, near-sighted decision-making is to be expected. It would be surprising if decisions were made differently.

One thing we know for sure, no organization in which self-interests dominate will ever realize its full potential. This is a critical challenge facing management. As Tommy Lasorda, former manager of the Los Angeles Dodgers, put it, "My responsibility is to get my twenty-five guys playing for the name on the front of their uniform and not the one on the back." [33]

To create this type of environment, two key changes will probably have to be made. The first is to change how performances are judged. Performances must be judged on the basis of the contribution individuals and departments are making to the company's goal of maximum sales. The second change is for all executives and managers to consider the impact field for all their decisions.

Few areas in society have enjoyed more dramatic advances than the field of medicine. Not only have there been astonishing improvements in the curing of diseases, but advances in their diagnosis have been equally revolutionary.

Medical diagnoses have advanced from the illness-focused procedures of yesterday to today's holistic approach that stresses consideration of the total person. This methodology is at once both curative and preventive for it addresses both curing the current ailment and preventing others in the future.

Most business organizations are remarkably similar to the human body in that a breakdown in one part affects the rest. Just as the holistic approach in medicine requires doctors to consider the entire person, when applied to a business, it requires that careful consideration be given to the entire organization prior to making any decision. This approach is critical to the attainment of a company's *Maximum Sales Potential*.

When a holistic approach is applied to the decision-making process, all the potential effects of a decision on other areas of the organization are considered prior to it being finalized. In a sales-friendly culture, particular attention will be given the effects on the Sales Department.

The executives and managers of every business are the linchpins to its success. As its leaders, they're in the position to establish holistic thinking as the standard throughout the organization. Once they do, the organization's operational efficiencies will begin improving immediately.

In addition to reducing inefficiencies that undermine sales performance, this approach will foster internal cooperation, improve morale and lead to more effective use of resources. As you'll see in Attribute #11, it will also help increase everyone's income.

As futile as it would be to run a business without using today's technologies, it is equally self-defeating to continue using the decision-making processes of yesteryear. Today's business world is far too demanding for any company to attempt to compete without first unifying its resources and energies. Adopting a holistic approach is a critical step towards that end.

It's the Sales Department's responsibility to present the company in the marketplace. Consequently, it's extremely vulnerable to any of the company's internal weaknesses. A holistic approach to decision-making will serve to limit those weaknesses and better enable the company to realize its *Maximum Sales Potential*.

THE HOLISTIC
DECISION-MAKING MODEL

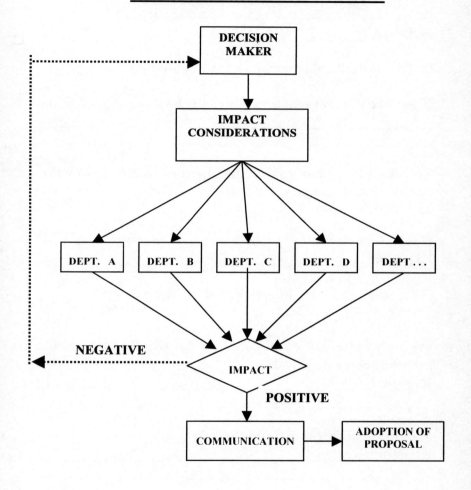

Attribute #8 Questionnaire

Do you consider each decision's impact field <u>before</u> you make it? _____

Is that a standard practice in your company? _____

What are the main factors you consider?

_____

_____

To what degree has your department been affected by the decisions of other departments?
No Impact   1   2   3   4   5   6   7   8   9   10   Major Impact

Has that impact more often been positive or negative?
Explain: _____

On a scale of 1 – 10, how political is the company?
Very Little   1   2   3   4   5   6   7   8   9   10   Major Factor

Would you like to see all decisions holistically evaluated before they're finalized? _____
Explain? _____

_____

Would that improve productivity? _____
Explain why: _____

_____

Would it save money / resources? _____
Explain: _____

_____

Do the needs of Sales affect your decisions? _____

Do you meet regularly with Sales managers? _____

114

Do you meet regularly with other managers to share information on proposed actions? _____

Do decisions made in your department do more to help or hurt company sales performance? _____
Explain: _____
_____

Could your department do more to help improve sales?
_____
Explain: _____
_____

If yes, are you planning on implementing the changes?
_____
When? _____

"Remember the Titanic! It's the things you don't see that'll sink your ship."

The Author

Attribute #9

Full Costs Are Always Considered

Business organizations have an almost boundless capacity for limiting their own success. The limitations they impose on themselves, however, aren't the product of some diabolical plot by disgruntled employees intent on sabotaging the company. To the contrary, most actually begin as good faith efforts to improve company performance.

Why then would good employees create situations that do so much damage to their own company? Although there are many answers to that question, I believe there are six primary reasons for the majority of inefficiencies. These are:

- Failure by individuals to fully consider the impact of their actions (procedures, activities etc.) on other people, other departments or company productivity.

- Internal Politics

- Competition between departments due in a large part to the structure of the internal organization

- Lack of any direct financial interest in the success of the company

- Failure to eliminate obsolete procedures or activities

- Unawareness of the actual costs of inefficiencies by the individuals creating them

The first three of these causes have been covered in previous segments, while the need for growth-based compensation is presented in-depth in Attribute #11. The issue of eliminating obsolete activities and procedures is addressed during the monthly department meetings mandated by the Program and outlined in Part III of this book.

That leaves lack of awareness of the actual costs as the final reason that inefficiencies are created. If employees were aware of their actual costs, most unproductive situations would quickly disappear. Unfortunately, few have been trained to think in terms of costs for their actions.

Calculating the costs of internal activities is a very inexact science. We're all familiar with the costs that are itemized on financial statements such as Operating Expenses, Interest Expense and Depreciation. The costs associated with unproductive activities, however, are usually anonymous.

These are what are commonly known as soft costs; costs not specifically itemized on the financial statements or normally recognized as costs by either employees or management. Nonetheless, they are costs and must be treated as such.

An example of a soft cost is the opportunity cost of an activity. If the returns realized from one activity are less than the potential returns from another, a loss is incurred for choosing the alternative with the lower return. These are known as the opportunity costs.

Opportunity costs are just one of any number of soft costs that must be considered before a policy, procedure or activity is adopted. Included among the most common soft costs are:

- **Costs in Time** – This is the actual dollar value of the time spent on an activity. The time costs associated with inefficiencies such as unnecessary meetings, needless procedures and policies, internal politics and the misuse of e-mail can be formidable.

- **Opportunity Costs** – As previously stated, this is the value of revenues that would have been generated had the time and energy expended on one activity been directed to an alternative, more productive activity. These are probably the most overlooked, and very often the greatest costs chargeable to internal inefficiencies.

- **Lost Customer Costs** – Inefficient operations always lead to lost customers. Most of the costs associated with losing any customer are soft and must include not only the revenues the departing customer was providing, but all of the costs incurred in replacing that customer with one of comparable purchasing and margin potential.

- **Costs of Resources** - All activities consume company resources. Inefficient ones, however, misuse them. This misuse can include everything from additional staffing needed to offset breakdowns in service to the ineffective use of phones, computers or postage.

  For example, when a company is consistently late with shipments, Customer Services must spend time responding to complaints and tracking shipments. This leads to longer waiting times for customers. The company can either suffer the loss of customers due to this degradation in service or it can increase its Customer Service staff. In either case, there are substantial costs to consider.

- **Morale Costs** – Unnecessary procedures, office politics and other inefficiencies frustrate productive individuals. Before long, the productivity levels of these employees are adversely affected. This decline in productivity is yet another soft cost that must be considered.

- **Turnover Costs** – Productive employees tend to leave unproductive environments for ones where their talents are better appreciated and rewarded. The loss of any quality worker is accompanied by an array of soft costs such as the lost productivity of the departing worker, the diminished productivity of those who must assume that person's workload, the cost of severance packages and the potential costs incurred when a productive worker is recruited by a competitor. These are in addition to the replacement costs cited in the next category on this list, Hiring Costs.

Turnover is one of the best barometers of the quality of a company's management. It's serves as a measure of many factors including: how effectively management is communicating, its success in challenging and motivating employees and even the degree to which it is trusted. Turnover is of such importance that it is Attribute #12 of the Program.

- **Hiring Costs** – An obvious consequence of turnover is the hiring costs of replacing departed workers. These include advertising for open positions, agency fees and time spent interviewing, selecting and assimilating the replacement workers.

- **Training Costs** – Costs associated with training new hires are another significant expense associated with an inefficient work environment.

- **Litigation Costs** – In today's litigious society, every business is at risk of legal action. Whether initiated by a disgruntled employee, customer or advocacy group, the costs can be substantial. The potential soft costs for legal problems can include a tainted public image, recruitment difficulties and productivity losses due to the internal turmoil such legal actions create.

There are no free lunches and there are no free inefficiencies. Each comes with costs that, although sometimes hidden, still inflict extensive damage to the bottom line of any company.

For a better idea of the subtlety of soft costs associated with common business activities, consider these examples:

- Sales meetings are a standard occurrence in business. When scheduled, only the costs of the meeting room and refreshments are normally considered. The actual costs, however, are far greater. For example, let's look at the costs in time for a two hour sales meeting. If a forty person sales force must travel one hour each way for a two hour meeting, the actual cost in time for the meeting is 160 sales hours. That's 10% of the sales force's work week which is the same as giving four salespeople the week off.

  When we add the opportunity and other resource costs (mileage, tolls, etc.) to the time costs, it's clear that a two hour meeting is far more expensive than first thought. It then seems reasonable to expect that before incurring such expenses, the person calling the meeting has determined that the content of the meeting will impact sales and revenue performance by an amount greater than its total cost.

- The costs associated with the use of e-mail also merit consideration. If we estimate that each manager and executive in a company receives fifty e-mails a day and each one takes two minutes to open, read, and generate a response, the leadership of the company is spending 100 minutes each day just on e-mail. That's 24% of their workday! If other employees receive only half that amount, they're spending fifty minutes or 12% of their workday on e-mail. That's not necessarily a bad thing. E-mail is an extremely valuable tool. Used effectively, it increases productivity and earnings. However, in light of the huge amount of resources it consumes, companies must ensure it is being used productively.

All that glitters is not gold. Inefficiencies sometimes come disguised as savings, when in fact their costs far exceed even their most generous savings estimates. Consider the following examples:

- Management chooses to rely on its sales force to search out new prospects instead of using an outside contractor. To determine the feasibility of this decision, all costs have to be considered. If a salesperson is earning $50,000 per year and uses two hours to find a viable prospect, the cost in time alone is $50 per lead. When travel and other related expenses of $5/hour are added, the cost rises to $60. If the salesperson's hourly net profit from sales is $50/hour, the opportunity cost is $100 bringing the total cost to $160/lead. Now, if the contractor's charge for each qualified lead is $40, the decision that was intended to provide savings is actually costing the company $120 for each lead generated by the sales force.

- To control costs, management decides to cap expenses at $300/month for all salespeople. This amount is to include all travel and entertainment expenses. Before finalizing this policy, the company must determine if the decision is prudent? For the answer, management must ask itself the following questions: Will the policy adversely affect the performance of the salespeople? Have the main competitors imposed similar restrictions? If not, will the policy put the company at a competitive disadvantage? What's the potential impact on revenues due to lost sales? Will productive salespeople leave the company for more generous settings?

Once again, the merits of each decision must be based on its total costs. If the revenue or savings realized exceed its total (both hard and soft) costs, the decision is a viable one. If not, the decision should be modified or rescinded.

As shown in these examples, money that isn't spent stays on the bottom line. This can be a strong inducement for managers to forego investments that don't hold the promise of immediate results. The pressures for immediate results from stockholders, the media and the general public only increase the temptation not to pursue these investments.

Companies must be careful not to sacrifice the future by letting these pressures obstruct their decision making. The soft costs (opportunity, morale, turnover, *et al*) inherent in such decisions are very difficult to accurately determine, however, a company's effort to save can easily result in unanticipated, anonymous losses.

Most of us rarely delve so deeply into our decisions. In fact, in some settings, internal influences place greater importance on the appearance of action than on actual results. In such a setting, the cosmetics of decision-making override the urgency for thorough evaluation.

Awareness of the costs associated with all internal operations is critically important to effective management. This won't happen by itself. Companies must actively train all employees, particularly their leaders, to accurately identify all costs associated with their decisions and to assess the merits of each decision accordingly. Such training will go a long way toward eliminating internal inefficiencies in the future.

As I've repeatedly stated, no company burdened with rampant inefficiencies will ever reach its full sales potential. For that reason alone, ensuring that each employee fully understands the obvious and the not so obvious costs of every activity is critical to successfully *Managing Your Business to Its Maximum Sales Potential.*

Attribute #9 Questionnaire

Did you consider the soft costs when making decisions prior to reading this segment? _____

Were you ever formally trained to recognize and estimate soft costs? _____
Explain: _____
_____

Do other managers normally consider soft costs? _____

Have decisions made by others departments imposed soft costs on your department? _____
Explain:_____
_____

Do other managers discuss their proposals with you, if they might affect your department? _____
Explain: _____

Should they? _____
Explain:_____
_____

Based on their soft costs, what recent decisions would you like to see changed? _____
_____

Are you under pressure for immediate results? _____
Explain: _____
_____

Can you think of other soft costs not cited in this chapter?
_____
_____

Will this help you make more effective decisions in the future? _____
How? _____

_____

_____

What are the soft costs associated with a new hire?

_____

_____

Calculate the soft costs of the last meeting you convened.

_____

_____

_____

"We must all hang together or assuredly,
we will all hang separately."

Benjamin Franklin

Attribute #10

All Employees are Familiar with the Demands of Selling

If you asked any salesperson what's the greatest challenge they face, they'll probably tell you its getting support from their own company. The reason that's the case is because in many companies an "us versus them" relationship exists between the internal organization and Sales.

Since most of the internal staff hasn't had any exposure to the selling experience, this isn't surprising. Having had no exposure, they are unaware of the difficulties involved in selling. Consequently, Sales is seen more as an inconvenience than the group charged with performing a vitally important function for the company.

Those of us who make our livelihood selling are all too familiar with its difficulties. The internal staff, however, has been insulated from the daily demands of customers. They haven't had to contend with customer threats to take their business elsewhere or the incessant demands for better pricing. They're unfamiliar with the letdown you feel when after months of hard work a prospect selects a competitor or when an established customer becomes disenchanted with your company's product or service. They also don't know what it's like to be hung out to dry when you're unable to get needed support from your own company.

This last point is critical. Every salesperson in the world is reliant on their internal staff for the support they need to effectively do their job. Without it, neither they nor the company has a hope of ever reaching its full potential.

I believe there are three key factors that contribute to the distance that exists between the internal organization and Sales in many companies. These are:

- As already stated, most members of the internal network on whom the salespeople are reliant for support are unfamiliar with the rigors and difficulties of selling. Forming their opinions strictly on external appearances, they tend to underestimate those demands.

- Customers and prospects are in a constant search for added value. Their demands force a company to change current policies and procedures. To the internal staff, this is often seen as a disruption to their orderly world and not as a vitally important activity for the continued growth and competitive health of the company. Since Sales serves as the messenger in this process, it's seen as the disruptive force.

- The third and probably most damaging reason is that management has permitted or even fostered a negative attitude towards Sales. As stated so many times before, the leaders of a company determine its culture. If they are supportive of Sales, the staff will follow. The inverse is also true. Management that is unsupportive gives license to an internal staff's uncooperative treatment of Sales. Without exception, an unfriendly sales culture spawns inflexibility, indifference, delays and an overall lack of cooperation that is so crucial to reaching the company's maximum sales potential. Although terribly self-defeating, you'd be amazed at how many members of the leadership ranks have been guilty of this through-out my career.

Sales aren't the only thing being lost. The constant search by customers for increased value is the catalyst that strengthens the competitive mettle of every business. It forces companies to accelerate their search for product or service improvements which, in turn, lead to advantages in the marketplace. Without customers to serve as the catalyst, the pace of such improvements would almost certainly slow. One of the greatest threats a negative view of Sales poses is that these demands are met with internal resistance, thereby, compromising the competitive strength of the business in the future.

For all of these reasons, eliminating negative attitudes towards Sales is critical to every company's sales performance. As with any cultural weakness, the first step in this process is recognition that a problem exists. The leadership must acknowledge that an unhealthy view of Sales exists within the organization and that only it has the authority and influence to change it.

The most immediate way to reverse this perception is for the leadership to alter its own view of Sales. Since the culture within a company reflects the view of its executives and managers, remarkable changes will occur when company's leaders voice and exhibit their support for the Sales.

Again, one of the main reasons internal support for Sales is frequently lacking is that most of those in supportive roles have never been exposed to the daily challenges of selling. In fact, most spend their entire careers never having been on a sales call, observed negotiations or even met with a customer face-to-face. How then could they possibly be expected to understand the critical importance their support plays in the sales performance of the company?

To correct this void, *Managing Your Business to Its Maximum Sales Potential* recommends that all members of the organization be acquainted with the selling experience. It is recommended that as part of the formal training process, each employee spend some time working directly with the Sales Department. This will ensure that all employees have had an opportunity to observe experienced salespeople as they prospect, resolve problems, prepare proposals, make presentations and perform all of the standard sales-related duties. The goal of this initiative is to engender a greater understanding of the intricacies of sales which, in turn, will improve both their appreciation of, and responsiveness to, the needs of the Sales Department.

The duration and format of this training would be at the discretion of the respective managers. The more frequently an individual is directly involved with either customers or salespeople, however, the greater the need for more extensive exposure.

Cooperation in all aspects of the sales process from entering orders to closing the sale is far too important to allow for culturally-induced disruptions. The benefits of this process of familiarizing everyone with the selling experience far outweigh any of its costs. Besides bringing the various segments of the organization closer, it will reinforce the philosophy that sales performance is the responsibility of each member of the organization. Everyone is a salesperson; attitudes change, barriers fall and resistance dissolves. With this initiative, the company is taking a huge step on the road to reaching its maximum sales potential.

Attribute #10 Questionnaire

On a scale of 1 – 10, how is the Sales Department viewed in your company?

<u>Favorable</u>   1   2   3   4   5   6   7   8   9   10   <u>Unfavorable</u>

What factors influence that perception?

_____

_____

Does that perception help or hurt the sales performance?
_____

Explain: _____

_____

Do you agree with the popular opinion? _____
Why? _____

_____

Who most influences the perception of Sales in the company? _____
How? _____

_____

Do you think the general perception of Sales accurately reflects its importance to the company? _____
Explain: _____

_____

How important is Sales to the company's success?

Irrelevant   1   2   3   4   5   6   7   8   9   10   Extremely
Explain: _____

_____

Which departments are more important than Sales?
_____
Why? _____
_____

Have you spent any time working with the salespeople?
_____

How much? _____

Have your people? _____

How would you improve the relationship between your department and Sales?
Explain:_____
_____

Do you think company sales performance would improve if the CEO and other leaders made it the top priority?

_____
Explain: _____
_____

Would sales performance improve if all employees were more familiar with the demands on sales and the needs of customers? _____
Explain: _____
_____
_____

What have you learned from this segment?
_____
_____
_____
_____

"Pay your people the least possible and you'll get from them the same."

Malcolm Forbes

"We're overpaying him, but he's worth it."

Samuel Goldwyn

Attribute #11

Compensation Structured for Sales Growth

Over the past three decades, the business environment has undergone remarkable cultural changes. Today's worker makes no bones about going to the highest bidder. Loyalty is based exclusively on how well their company meets their personal and financial needs.

On the other hand, companies have responded in kind. The lifelong interest they once showed for their workers, such as IBM's commitment of a "job for life," is but a distant memory. Pensions have been revised downward, education benefits eliminated and employees must now contribute to their medical coverage. All clearly indicate that company interests override those of the workers.

This polarization has become even more pronounced with recent revelations of the blatant misuse of authority for personal gain by so many executives. Shenanigans at Enron, Tyco, Arthur Anderson, Global Crossing *et al* have served to further justify the priority employees now place on their own self-interests.

It's very hard to say which came first, the chicken or the egg. Did workers disconnect first or did the companies? The answer is irrelevant. What's relevant is that this distance between companies and their workers exists. Leadership is in the unenviable position of having to find ways to bridge that distance so their entire organization can work as a cohesive, goal-oriented unit. Clearly, old-time remedies won't suffice.

135

First on the minds of all workers is compensation. It's also an area that has lagged the trend of change. The formula for calculating compensation has remained virtually unchanged for years. Companies continue to offer a salary with benefits and, if they can't be avoided, annual increases. Whether a worker performs at 80% or 100% makes little difference. Additionally, political and budgetary forces stand guard over current policies and thwart any suggestion of change. Clinging to old paradigms in a world that is changing with the speed of light is a prescription for lost opportunities or, worse yet, total failure.

All these convergent forces place management between a rock and a hard place. While everyone wants exceptional performance, current compensation philosophies don't foster it.

Since the objective for a company is to reach its *Maximum Sales Potential*, it stands to reason that its compensation plan should be structured to support that goal. If we agree that the company's sales performance is the responsibility of every employee, then we should also agree that every employee must share financially in the results of those efforts.

Lou Gerstner saw this connection between compensation and results as he worked to unify and transform IBM. "Nothing was more important to fostering a one-for-all team environment than a common incentive compensation opportunity for large numbers of IBMers – an opportunity that was heavily dependent on how the overall corporation performed."[34]

Clearly, businesses must rethink the current compensation paradigm. Innovative approaches to compensation must be formulated and pursued.

Like Social Security is to politicians, compensation is the political third rail in most companies. Changing it in any way will require courage, but then again, *Managing Your*

Business to Its Maximum Sales Potential will only be pursued by individuals and organizations with the will and courage to embrace needed change.

Vibrant, competitive companies adjust to change.   It's foolish to think that today's employees will stretch to their maximum potential without personal financial gain.   Any company that fails to recognize this will remain mired in the blasé world of mediocre results.

Sam Walton, arguably the most successful retailer in the history of America, affirmed his belief in performance-based compensation with his admission, "the single biggest regret in my whole business career is that we didn't include our associates in the initial, managers-only profit sharing plan when we took the company public in 1970."   It took Mr. Walton only one year to realize the error of his ways.   The following year, all associates were included in the plan. [35]

He had come to the realization that, "the more you share profits with your associates – whether it's in salaries or incentives or bonuses or stock discounts - the more profits they will accrue to the company." [36]   His philosophy was simple: "The way management treats associates is exactly how the associates will then treat the customers.   And if the associates treat the customers well, the customers will return again and again, and that is where the real profit in business lies.   Satisfied, loyal, repeat customers are at the heart of Wal-Mart's spectacular profit margins, and those customers are loyal because our associates treat them better than salespeople in other stores do. [37]

For the first twenty years (1971 - 1990) after the profit-sharing plan was expanded to include all associates, sales jumped a whopping 839 times from $31 million to $26 billion.   This was certainly due to a large extent to the opening of 1,496 Wal-Mart stores during that period, however the effect of expanding the profit-sharing plan to all employees is best evidenced in its per store sales which increased over 17 times during the same period. Most astoundingly, this growth was attained with no decline in Wal-Mart's profit margin! [38]

In 2003, Sam Walton's philosophy of sharing the company's financial success with all its employees was formally recognized when Wal-Mart received the #1 ranking on both the *Fortune* 500 and the *Fortune* List of Most Admired Companies. Wal-Mart is the first company to be simultaneously ranked #1 on both lists.[39] Walton understood that employees are motivated by the ability to improve their lot in life.

> **The wise man understands equity; the small man understands only profits.**
>
> **Confucius**

A company will be positioned for maximum sales only after it has found a way to share its success directly with those individuals who have created it – its employees. To effectively do this, that plan must do the following:

1. Promote total cooperation within the organization

2. Focus the entire organization on the goal of reaching its maximum sales potential

3. Attain profit growth comparable to the growth in sales

Sharing the financial gains of the company with every employee is one of the linchpins of *Managing Your Business to Its Maximum Sales Potential*. For that purpose, a plan known as Shared Burden/Shared Reward has been developed. This plan satisfies the requirement for sharing in the sales growth revenues, while also successfully satisfying the three listed criteria of an effective compensation plan.

Under this Plan, gross sales targets are established each month. The target is set at 5% above the gross sales for the same month the previous year plus the CPI for the previous year. For example, if last June's gross sales were $100,000 and the CPI for the year was 4%, the target for this June would be $109,000.

When sales reach that figure, a percentage (3% - 4%) of all additional sales for the month is set aside and put into what is known as the company's "Sales Growth Fund." At the end of the month, the contents of this fund are distributed equally among all <u>non-Sales</u> personnel. This will ensure that every member of the organization has a vested interest in its continuous sales growth. The greater the sales level, the greater the bonus.

To be effective, every member of the organization must have total confidence in the integrity of the Shared Burden/Shared Reward Plan. To that end, it must be designed along the following guidelines:

- The plan must be tamperproof. Shared Burden/Shared Reward is a pact between the company and its employees and cannot be modified in response to the changing economic needs of the organization.

- Targets must be attainable.

- The formula for assigning targets and payments, once established, cannot change.

- To attain its desired effect, the participants must see frequent payouts at regular intervals. Longer payout periods would leave the company vulnerable to manipulation and lessen the enthusiasm for the plan. In light of these considerations, monthly performance payments are strongly recommended.

- The target must be communicated to all employees at the beginning of each month. It is also recommended that the running total of sales be tracked and communicated throughout the month. Effective communication is a key element to maintaining employee momentum.

As noted, salespeople and sales managers are excluded from the Shared Burden/Shared Reward plan. They will operate under a separate, uncapped commission plan that pays progressively higher rates as individual sales volumes increase.

Commissions are one of management's most effective tools for improving sales force productivity. Despite its usefulness in affecting desired outcomes, companies continue to design plans in ways that actually limit sales performance. Sometimes this is done by capping earnings above a certain level of sales which all but ensures the performance of every salesperson will decline once that level is reached. Companies with uncapped plans frequently avoid increasing commission rates as sales increase. If these companies provided a progressive commission schedule, they would be giving all of their salespeople, particularly top sales producers, the incentive necessary to keep them focused and productive through the end of the year.

Managing Your Business to Its Maximum Sales Potential must include a compensation plan that promotes maximum sales performance. To that end, it must be structured so that the more the company sells, the more the employees earn. Since increases in compensation are always accompanied by corresponding increases in company earnings, there is never a need to apply a ceiling to individual earnings under the Shared Burden/Shared Reward plan.

A key to leading a company to its maximum sales potential is allowing all parties involved in the effort the opportunity to maximize their incomes. To expect to reach that objective without providing that opportunity is an admission that the company is satisfied with its current performance. In any business climate, that attitude can be fatal.

Managing Your Business to Its Maximum Sales Potential represents a break with traditional thinking. A company's compensation plan is the roadmap to attaining its objectives. If reaching its maximum sales potential is that objective, a company must design its compensation plan in such a way that all of its employees are driving in that direction.

Attribute #11 Questionnaire

How are employees rewarded for sales growth?
Bonus _____ **Profit Sharing** _____
Salary Increase _____ **No Reward** _____
Other _____ **Explain:** _____

Is sales growth the top priority for most managers? _____
Explain: _____
_____

Is sales growth the top priority for most employees? _____
Explain: _____
_____

Are you concerned with company sales performance?
Explain: _____
_____

Is there a correlation between income and sales growth?
Explain: _____
_____

If sales grow, do you benefit financially? _____

Does this affect you concern with sales growth? _____

As sales grow, does your workload increase? _____
_____

Who designed the compensation plan in your company?
_____

Can you do anything to increase your income?
Explain: _____
_____

If you could, would your productivity increase? _____
Explain: _____
_____

Would you like to have uncapped earnings potential?
Explain why: _____
_____

On a scale of 1 – 10, how do you feel when company sales
increase?
Indifferent   1   2   3   4   5   6   7   8   9   10   Extremely Pleased

Why? _____
_____

How do members of the internal organization feel when
sales increase?
Indifferent   1   2   3   4   5   6   7   8   9   10   Extremely Pleased

Why? _____
_____

Should the compensation plan be revised? _____
How? _____
_____
_____

"A company can spend its time and resources replacing lost workers or it can spend them generating sales and profits. It can't do both!"

The Author

Attribute #12

Low Turnover

As a fellow manager used to say, "Turnover is a very expensive hobby!" Losing productive employees is one of the most destructive and costly problems any business can have. In addition to the loss of qualified workers, there are the associated issues of interrupted productivity, replacement costs (screening training, processing etc.), costs in time, redistributed workloads and most damaging of all, the message it sends to every employee in the organization.

Another frequently overlooked cost is the high probability a company's turnover is an attractive recruitment opportunity for competitors. People who leave a company are going somewhere. Very often, they end up working for one of the competitors, who are only too happy to welcome them into their organizations.

Before looking for remedies, I think it best if we determine why people leave companies in the first place? Some, of course, leave for personal reasons. Most, however, leave because their company is not adequately meeting their needs. Since people rarely leave without first giving some signals regarding their intentions, the departure of most is avoidable.

People don't leave environments where their skills are tested, their contributions appreciated and their need for belonging is being fulfilled. They leave when the situation they're in doesn't adequately challenge their talents, makes them feel unappreciated or reeks with intrigue and distrust.

I've always found that environments dominated by politics are plagued by unusually high turnover. In such a setting, a caste system of "innies" and "outies" prevails. The ruling class, the "innies," although in the minority, dominates all internal activities. Status as opposed to performance is the measure of importance. Not surprisingly, those employees choosing not to play the game or who are not afforded rank by the "innies" usually end up leaving for more hospitable environs.

Whether it's to a competitor or to a new industry, the loss of any productive employee is a setback. When this happens, management must ask itself how it failed to provide an environment in which a qualified, productive individual wanted to remain and grow.

Once again, the leaders within a company establish its environment and culture. They decide who joins the company, who stays, how they're compensated, how resources are used, what company goals are and how those goals will be achieved. It is therefore their duty to ensure that the company's environment and culture adequately meet the needs of its employees so that turnover doesn't drain the organization of valuable talent.

When individuals rise to management positions, they must have the communications and people skills needed to lead. Unfortunately, that's not always the case. In fact, very often the exit interview is the first time many employees have the opportunity to discuss their needs, hopes and dreams with their manager.

Nothing creates turnover more quickly than an unqualified manager. Everyone has a story about a manager from hell. I worked with one fellow who had never managed during an economic slowdown. Politics was his craft in trade.

As sales dropped, he would get steadily angrier. This guy would get so angry, he actually changed colors. His inability to effectively respond to the difficult conditions victimized everyone in his group.

146

If he had been experienced, he would have known that the conditions called for strict adherence to the sound principles of selling. Well-planned prospecting, thorough preparation, responsiveness to customers and maximized "selling time" would have the best chance of delivering the desired results.

He also would have realized his people were looking for his support and guidance. Instead, he embarked on a reign of terror treating his charges as if they were responsible for the downturn in the economy.

With each passing week, he unwound a little more. His lack of leadership skills were clearly evidenced in a threatening memo he sent to the members of his team stating, "I had better start to see marked improvement with members of this team. In case you didn't notice, our numbers stink, and stink runs downhill."

The company paid a tremendous price for its promotion of someone so unsuited for a leadership role. In just a few months, employees representing over 100 years of selling experience and 50 years of tenure left the company. Not until an employee survey was conducted, however, did his managers even realize what was happening.

Unfortunately, the damage had already been done. The costs to the company in lost opportunities, HR issues, lowered morale, severance packages, hiring, training, assimilating replacements, and litigation risks far exceeded anything this guy could possibly offer the organization.

In retrospect, what was management thinking? After all, they selected him for that position. How could they have overlooked the absence of such critical traits as experience, people skills and professionalism in promoting an individual like this?

147

Richard McGinn, former CEO of Lucent Technologies, exhibited similar behavior when faced with bad news. When Nina Aversano, Lucent's top sales executive, notified him on a conference call that "orders were drying up, major customers were cutting spending, and even the recently reduced sales projections for the quarter would be missed, McGinn 'went ballistic,' . . . and sent his sales team into a frenzy of last minute wheeling and dealing to make the numbers.

The frenzy produced - or appeared to produce - what the boss had demanded: Lucent missed its quarter by less than 2 percent." [40]

The sales results, however, were not without a price. "Lucent had given lavish credits and discounts to pull sales into the quarter, thereby stealing from the future to meet McGinn's demands in the present. *The Wall Street Journal* added, 'It booked sales for goods that were shipped to distribution channels . . . and improperly booked some sales that never qualified as revenue'." [41]

Shortly thereafter, Aversano informed McGinn that because of "the effects of all these tricks," Lucent would miss its 2001 sales goals by 20%. She accused him of setting "hopelessly optimistic" sales targets and resigned. Two weeks later, McGinn was fired by the board. She (Aversano) filed suit against the company alleging "she was forced to resign for telling the truth about Lucent's misstatements and mismanagement." [42]

As it turned out, Aversano's projections were off. Sales for 2001 dropped 26%. [43]

I seriously doubt that the 2000 downturn in sales was McGinn's first lapse in managerial decorum. Over the years, I'm sure his limitations were there for everyone to see.

Unfortunately for Lucent and its many employees, no one saw or wanted to see them.

In both these cases, qualified, proven employees left their company. Was either of these individuals looking out for the best interests of their companies or themselves?

If a company wants to squander its resources, there's no better way than to increase turnover. And if a company wants a high turnover rate, all it has to do is promote individuals who lack the ability, experience or demeanor to assume the responsibilities of leadership.

The litmus test that should be applied by management before any individual is considered for a leadership role is, "Would I trust this individual with my son or daughter's career?" If not, don't promote. If yes, you probably have an individual who will be a productive and stabilizing influence for the organization – a leader.

Despite the devastation it can wreak on a business, turnover doesn't usually command the attention it warrants. In fact, it's frequently viewed by managers as more of a political than a productivity issue. This is due in large part to the fact that the costs associated with turnover aren't specifically identified on any financial statements. This anonymity all but eliminates any direct internal accountability.

I have always felt that some uniform estimate of turnover tracking should be adopted and used to measure management performance. If such a system were adopted, turnover would be viewed quite differently. Managers would begin taking greater care in hiring, motivating, communicating and caring for the members of their team.

For arguments sake, let's say an assessment of $40,000 is entered in a manager's record for each employee who resigns after two or more years of service. Additionally, a charge in

149

the same amount would be made against the company's earnings. In other words, if three people resign, the manager's record would indicate $120,000 in turnover charges. The company's off-book earnings would also be reduced by that same amount. Turnover would then be given a much higher priority among the leaders of the company.

All resources are finite, especially people. To minimize the threat that turnover poses to every business, the *Managing Your Business to Its Maximum Sales Potential* Program recommends that participating companies adopt the following two initiatives

- Implementation of a cost-based system for measuring turnover on both a company and individual manager basis.

- Establish a policy that any person being considered for a leadership role must be interviewed and evaluated by no fewer than three current leaders.

No company that has a constant rotation of personnel will ever reach its full sales potential. The loss of good people is much too important an issue to be overlooked. The adoption of these two recommended initiatives will help insulate a company against the loss of its most valuable resource – its people.

<u>Attribute #12 Questionnaire</u>

What's your company's annual turnover rate? _____%

What's the turnover rate in your department? _____%

How many employees have left your department in the past year? _____

What's the main reason people left your department?
_____

Other reasons: _____
_____

How often do you meet with them individually to discuss their feelings, expectations, and concerns?
Never__Annually__Quarterly __Monthly __ Weekly ___

Do you think that's sufficient? _____

How often do your manager meet with you?
Never__Annually__Quarterly __Monthly __ Weekly ___

Do you feel that's sufficient? _____

What are the main concerns of your employees?
_____

What do employees like best about your company?
_____

How important is retention of productive employees in your company?
<u>Unimportant</u>   1   2   3   4   5   6   7   8   9   10   Very <u>Important</u>

What is the most difficult aspect of replacing employees who leave?

_____

What costs does the company incur when a good employee leaves? (Be specific)

_____

_____

If you were held accountable for those costs, would you be more responsive to employee concerns? _____
Explain: _____

On a scale of 1 – 10, how would you rate your ability to retain productive workers?

<u>Poor</u>   1 2 3 4 5 6 7 8 9 10   <u>Excellent</u>

If you could change anything in the company, what would it be?

_____

What are you doing to help bring about these changes?

_____

If these changes were made, would fewer people leave?

_____

Who in the organization controls these conditions?

_____

PART III

THE IMPLEMENTATION:
MAKING THE PROGRAM A REALITY

"Plans without action produce nothing."

                                    The Author

Program Implementation

Every New Year we promise to rid ourselves of all our bad habits. Despite the fact they've been embedded for years, we vow to cleanse ourselves "cold turkey." In just a few short days, however, their gravitational pull exerts itself and we return to our bad old ways.

One of the main reasons this annual ritual ends in failure so often is its revolutionary nature. Change that produces long-term results is almost always evolutionary; carefully planned and consistently adopted over time. *Managing Your Business to Its Maximum Sales Potential* is designed to follow such a gradual schedule.

This Program consists of two separate, yet cooperative initiatives. The first entails the elimination of all internal inefficiencies – those situations and activities that consume valuable resources and energy, yet contribute nothing to the company's sales or earnings performance. All employees will participate directly in this process.

The second initiative calls for the company's adoption of twelve separate qualities. Known collectively as the Twelve Attributes, each has been selected to strengthen one of a business organization's critical performance elements. This initiative will be coordinated and overseen by the Efficiency Council, a separate committee established specifically for that purpose. The Efficiency Council is explained in detail in Step 4 of the next section, The Introduction Phase.

Both initiatives complement each other. The elimination of inefficiencies frees a company's internal resources to focus on improving its sales performance. The Twelve Attributes, meanwhile, will position the organization for maximum performance, while also lessening the possibility that new inefficiencies will be adopted in the future.

Implementation of the entire Program is a twelve step process (not to be confused with the Twelve Attributes). The initial eight steps comprise the Introduction Phase. Once completed, these steps will only be repeated on an as-needed basis. The remaining four steps, collectively known as the Continuous Improvement Phase, will be repeated monthly. The twelve steps of the Implementation are as follows:

THE INTRODUCTION PHASE

1. **Recognition by the CEO That a Problem Exists**
2. **Commitment to the Program by the CEO**
3. **Enlisting Company Leadership**
4. **Establishing the Efficiency Council**
5. **Training Company Leaders**
6. **Planning and Scheduling Program Introduction**
7. **Announcement to All Employees**
8. **Program Initiation**

THE CONTINUOUS IMPROVEMENT PHASE

9. **Monthly Department Meetings**
10. **Submission of Monthly Efficiency Reports**
11. **Council Progress Assessment and Adjustment**
12. **Council Communication Updates**

THE IMPLEMENTATION PROCESS

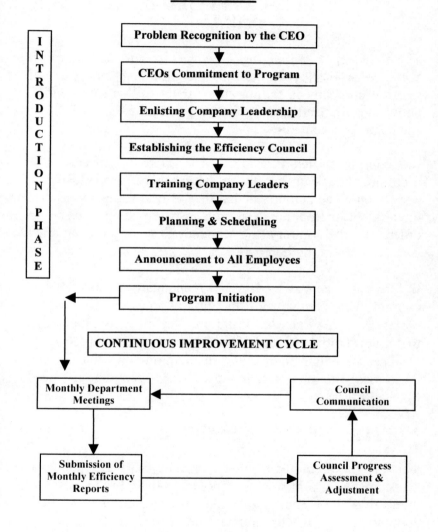

INTRODUCTION PHASE

Problem Recognition by the CEO

↓

CEOs Commitment to Program

↓

Enlisting Company Leadership

↓

Establishing the Efficiency Council

↓

Training Company Leaders

↓

Planning & Scheduling

↓

Announcement to All Employees

↓

Program Initiation

CONTINUOUS IMPROVEMENT CYCLE

Monthly Department Meetings

Council Communication

Submission of Monthly Efficiency Reports

Council Progress Assessment & Adjustment

THE INTRODUCTION PHASE

1. <u>RECOGNITION BY THE CEO THAT A PROBLEM EXISTS</u>

The first step to *Managing Your Business to Its Maximum Sales Potential* is recognition by the CEO or business owner that the company is falling short of its full sales potential. Only after the leader recognizes a problem exists will he or she be open to remedies.

Realizing that sales are being lost to internal inefficiecies or a culture that is unfriendly to sales can be a very difficult admission. The paradox is that the better a company's sales, the less apt its leaders are to even suspect that changes are in order. To the contrary, the tendency is to become satisfied with the current methods.

Before any business leaders can realistically be expected to commit their company to an initiative as extensive as the *Maximum Sales Potential* Program, they must first recognize that a substantial volume of sales are currently being lost to weaknesses within their own organization. For that reason, the critical first step is helping the CEO recognize the need for the Program.

2. <u>COMMITMENT TO THE PROGRAM BY THE CEO</u>

This Program requires resources and the full participation of all segments of a business. Since only the CEO or business owner has the authority to make such a commitment, their endorsement of the Program is the critical next step in the process.

In addition to the breadth of the Program, the CEO or owner also must fully understand that the Program is fully never completed. Internal processes will be under continuous scrutiny and each of the Twelve Attributes will be consistently monitored and refined in response to new opportunities for improvement, changing trends, or myriad other internal and external factors.

Therefore, the next step is to ensure the CEO understands the demands of the Program and commits the full participation and cooperation of the entire organization.

3. ENLISTING COMPANY LEADERSHIP

All executives and managers must understand their critical importance to the success of the Program. As the leaders within the company, these are the individuals who will oversee the introduction, implementation and management of the Program. It's their leadership that others will follow. It's their expertise that will give the Program its structure. It's their example that will set the tone for the level of enthusiasm and participation throughout the company. For all of these reasons, enlisting their support is the critical third step in the process.

4. ESTABLISHING THE EFFICIENCY COUNCIL

A central authority is needed to oversee the management and ongoing progress of the Program. To that end, the Efficiency Council will be established. Comprised of individuals selected by the CEO from the executive and senior management ranks, the Council will consist of one representative from each of the company's critical disciplines. An administrator will also be assigned to the Council to coordinate and complete its administrative duties.

Although the number of departments will vary by company, no more than one representative from each will be on the Council. The Efficiency Councils in most companies will probably include representatives from the following areas:

Finance (Credit, Accounts Receivable and Payable)
Sales
Administrative Services
Human Resources
Information Systems
Legal
Customer Services
Purchasing
Operations (Warehouse, Transportation, Manufacturing)
Advertising & Marketing

Council responsibilities include the following:

- Overseeing Program implementation
- Monitoring Program progress
- Evaluating departmental initiatives
- Recommending enhancements
- Reporting Program progress to the CEO
- Communicating Program issues and initiatives to the employee population
- Overseeing the changes necessary for integration of the Twelve Attributes.

The Attributes will require a variety of organization-wide changes. Some, such as adopting a sales-friendly culture and employing a holistic approach to decision-making are behavioral. These will require the cooperation of every employee and the consistent reinforcement by management.

Others, such as revamping the compensation plan and establishing the financial measurements for turnover are structural and will require final approval by the CEO. The Council will be responsible for designing and implementing such structural changes.

Each department manager will provide the Council with a monthly report on the efficiency initiatives taking place in their area. The Council will review these initiatives, track their progress and make recommendations as needed. These will then be summarized and communicated to all employees in a monthly communiqué generated by the Council.

5. <u>TRAINING COMPANY LEADERS</u>

To successfully implement the *Maximum Sales* Program, all company leaders must have both a complete understanding of the Program's Twelve Attributes and the ability to effectively recognize and reverse internal inefficiencies. To gain these skills, each will be required to attend a 3 day training seminar.

The seminar will consist of four sessions:

Session 1 – Overview of the Program:
> Explain Program objectives, define its benefits and outline the role it will play in ensuring the continuous growth and health of the company

Session 2 – Review the Twelve Attributes:
> Highlight the specific purpose of each Attribute, review the Attribute integration process and explain the critical importance the executives and managers play in the successful integration and acceptance of the Attributes

Session 3 – Review of Internal Inefficiencies:
> Define the varieties of inefficiencies, review methods for correcting them, perform exercises to assist in recognizing them, explain the concept of the *impact field* of decisions and hold group discussions on the causes and remedies for inefficiencies.

Session 4 –Explanation of Responsibilities and Duties:
Define roles and responsibilities of company leaders, review objectives of the monthly departmental meetings, discuss ways to encourage enthusiasm for the Program and foster active participation in the meetings and review the format for the Monthly Reports to the Efficiency Council.

Members of the Efficiency Council will have an additional one day training session to address Council responsibilities including Program planning and scheduling, designing and introducing the various Attributes, evaluating initiatives submitted by individual departments, monitoring the progress of the Program and communicating that progress to the CEO and the employee population.

6. PLANNING & SCHEDULING THE PROGRAM INTRODUCTION

The Efficiency Council is charged with responsibility for developing the plan and schedule for introduction of the Program. It will also establish the format for submission of the monthly updates on improved efficiencies from each department.

The department managers will set the schedule for monthly meetings. The monthly departmental meetings (Step 9) should begin immediately after the Council has distributed the appropriate form for the monthly departmental updates.

Before any of the Twelve Attributes can be addressed, the Council must first evaluate current operations to determine to what extent, if any, they currently exist. Only then will the Council be in a position to effectively proceed with designing each in concert with the requirements of the Program. In the preparation of each Attribute, the Council will work directly with the CEO, whose approval is required before its formal adoption.

Once the schedule and plans have been defined by the Council, the Program will be introduced to all members of the organization.

7. <u>ANNOUNCEMENT TO ALL EMPLOYEES</u>

Announcing the Program to all employees is the next step in the process. This announcement of the Program involves two separate presentations:

<u>PRESENTATION 1</u>

1. The CEO announces maximum sales performance as the overriding goal for the company and the expectation that each employee assume responsibility for achieving that objective.

2. The CEO announces the adoption of the *Maximum Sales Potential* Program and provides an overview of the objectives, compensation enhancements and the development of a sales-focused culture throughout the company – one in which every employee is an active participant in the company's sales efforts.

3. Creation of the Efficiency Council is announced and its members are introduced.

4. The ranking member of the Council will provide an overview of the mechanics of the system, while reiterating the CEO's message that the success of the Program is contingent on full participation by every employee.

PRESENTATION II

Each department manager will then meet with their staff. It's recommended that a member of the Council be in attendance during these sessions to reinforce the unified support for the Program.

During these sessions, the Program will be explained as it applies to the respective department. The meeting schedule and details of the compensation plan will also be presented. It's recommended that the manager afford the group ample time for Q & A. It's critically important that all questions/issues be addressed immediately and forthrightly during this initial meeting.

8. PROGRAM INITIATION

The Initiation Phase marks the formal start of Program activities. Sales levels at this time will be the benchmark for measuring future effectiveness of the Program. It also marks the start of both the sales-based compensation plan and the monthly efficiency meetings in each department.

During this Phase, it is especially important that all leaders stay on message emphasizing the company's "sales-focused" attitude to all employees. Employees should begin thinking of ways to best improve company sales performance and how they can contribute to that end. This effort will accelerate the Program's progress as managers continue to stress the need for active participation.

This is the final step in the Introduction Phase. Each of the eight steps in this Phase will be repeated only when needed. As shown in the schematic of the Implementation Process on page 157, Steps (9 – 12) are the Continuous Improvement Phase of the Program. This Phase is ongoing with each step being repeated on a regular basis.

THE CONTINUOUS IMPROVEMENT PHASE

9. MONTHLY DEPARTMENT MEETINGS

The vehicle for ensuring total employee participation in the Program is the monthly efficiency meeting. Each department will meet monthly to exchange ideas and submit suggestions on ways to improve departmental and company efficiency. The format of the meeting is determined by the department manager.

To promote a free and open sharing of ideas, an informal air to these meetings is recommended. An administrator should be assigned to take notes and keep a record of all suggestions and initiatives.

10. SUBMISSION OF MONTHLY EFFICIENCY REPORTS

Following each meeting, the department manager will then submit a formal report to the Efficiency Council listing the highlights of the meeting and the initiatives the department will be undertaking over the next month. The report must also include an update on the status of previous initiatives. The manager of the department is responsible for personally preparing and submitting this report to the Council.

11. COUNCIL PROGRESS ASSESSMENT & UPDATE

During the Assessment and Update phase, the progress of the Program is evaluated and measured by the Efficiency Council. The Council reviews all the departmental information that has been gathered and makes recommendations to each respective department manager. The Council also evaluates the progress of the Program and communicates its findings to the CEO and the employee community.

This stage consists of six critical steps:

1) Collection of the Monthly Efficiency Reports.
2) Evaluation of improved efficiency initiatives
3) Submission of recommendations to each department
4) Measurement of sales against the benchmark
5) Evaluation of progress in the integration of the Twelve Attributes
6) Reassessment of the Program's Schedule

The Assessment and Update stage provides the rudder for the Program. Without these monthly evaluations, the Council would be unable to effectively guide the company to the attainment of its *Maximum Sales Potential.*

12. COUNCIL COMMUNICATION UPDATES

The Program's success is dependent on the participation of all employees. Consistent communication is critical to attaining that level of involvement. Each person must know and understand every aspect of the Program. Since each employee will now be sharing financially in the company's growth, they will react immediately to the guidance provided by the Council.

Following completion of its evaluations, the Council will communicate its findings and all other Program-related information to the employee population. A monthly update from the Council will be created for that purpose.

Since organizations vary in size, communications can pose logistical problems. E-mail is a convenient and inexpensive way for getting the information to most members of the organization. Each department manager must ensure that those employees without access to the company e-mail system receive hardcopy versions of these updates.

Momentum is one of the key factors to the success of this Program. This only accentuates the need for consistent, thorough updates. To help maintain the continuity of the Program, each department meeting should open with a review of the Council's most recent update.

The process of *Managing Your Business to Its Maximum Sales Potential* is relatively straightforward and simple. The greatest obstacle that companies face will be overcoming organizational complacency.

Insanity has been defined as continuously doing the same thing yet expecting a different result. If a company wants to maximize its performance, it must do things differently. The principles of *Managing Your Business to Its Maximum Sales Potential* can be that difference. The choice is yours.

Any company with the foresight to adopt and vigorously pursue this Program will be well on its way to reaching its *Maximum Sales Potential.*

THE EFFICIENCY EVALUATION PROCESS

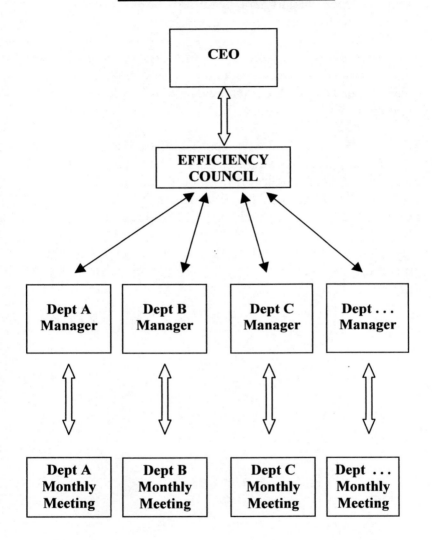

IN CLOSING

My objective in writing this book was to formulate my professional experiences into an organized Program by which businesses can reach their full potential. I'm confident that any business that adopts and maintains its commitment to the *Maximum Sales Potential* Program will enjoy a remarkable improvement in its sales and earnings growth.

The Program itself is simple; not easy, but simple. When you consider that the changes prescribed don't require any action beyond a company's front door, you realize the extent to which businesses currently limit their own performance. Since lost productivity is almost always self-inflicted, it's clearly within the control of the companies themselves to modify or reverse it.

Business organizations make choices. If a business is inefficient or lacks focus, its leaders have made that choice. If, on the other hand, a business is efficient, competitive and successful, its leaders have also made those choices. This Program, *Managing Your Business to Its Maximum Sales Potential,* is just such a choice.

Corporations are not by themselves animate objects. It's the people that give them life. People give them their personality. It's those same people who with proper guidance bring a company to its maximum potential.

To do that, they must have capable leadership, a sense of oneness and an opportunity to share in the company's financial success. As stressed throughout this book, the performance of every business is a reflection of its leaders. They're the only ones with the authority necessary to create such an environment. When they make the proper choices, the full participation and commitment of every employee is certain to follow.

Managing Your Business to Its Maximum Sales Potential is really a Program in organizational behavior. In adopting its principles, a business directs the behaviors of its employees so collectively they reach their maximum potential. The principles of the Program are universal. When applied to any organization, it will become more efficient. They are also timeless. They would have generated the same productivity improvements in Ancient Rome as they will today.

Attaining its *Maximum Sales Potential* is within the reach of every company. CEOs shouldn't be asking themselves whether or not they can afford to make such a far-reaching commitment for their company.

The question really is, "Can we afford not to?"

ENDNOTES

[1] Dell, Michael, <u>Direct from Dell</u>, (New York, 1999), p. 128.
[2] Charan, Ram and Tichy, Noel, <u>Every Business is a Growth Business</u>, (New York, 1998), p. 22.
[3] "Sales Help Drive Market's Biggest Winners." <u>Investors Business Daily</u>, October 24, 2000, p. 1
[4] Goodman, Ted ed., <u>The Forbes Book of Business Quotations</u>, (New York, 1997), p. 734.
[5] Neff, John. <u>John Neff on Investing</u>, (New York, 1999), p. 79.
[6] Moore, Edwin, ed., <u>Collins Gem Quotations</u> (Glasgow, 1961), p.139
[7] Canaday, Henry, "Compaq in Command," <u>Selling Power</u>, Vol. 18#5, (June 1998), pp. 55 – 61.
[8] National Commission on Excellence in Education, <u>A Nation at Risk: The Imperative for Educational Reform</u>. Washington D.C., U.S. Government Printing Office, April, 1983.
[9] Ibid., p. 20.
[10] Esquith, Rafe, <u>There are No Shortcuts</u>, (New York, 2003), Leaf.
[11] "Expectations May Alter Outcomes Far More Than We Realize." <u>The Wall Street Journal</u>, p. B1.
[12] Underwood, Jim, <u>More than a Pink Cadillac</u>, (New York, 2003), p. x.
[13] Collins, Jim, <u>Good to Great</u>, (New York, 2001), p. 91.
[14] Mickey Mantle, <u>The Education of a Baseball Player</u>, (New York, 1969), p. 42 – 43.
[15] Robert Slater, <u>Jack Welch and the GE Way</u> (New York, 1999), p. 35.
[16] Ibid., p. 38-39.
[17] Peter F. Drucker, <u>The Effective Executive</u> (New York, 1966), p.5-6.
[18] Collins, Jim, <u>Good to Great</u>, (New York, 2001), p. 1.
[19] Gerstner, Louis, <u>Who Says Elephants Can't Dance</u>, (New York, 2002), p. 117.
[20] Ibid. p. 184-185.
[21] Grosvenor, Edwin and Wesson, Morgan, <u>Alexander Graham Bell</u>, (New York, 1997), p. 75.
[22] Campbell, Malcolm, "The Best Manager in America," <u>Selling Power</u>, (Jan/Feb 1999), p. 53.
[23] Ibid.
[24] Ibid. p. 53.
[25] Murphy, Richard, "Profile: Michael Dell," <u>Success</u>, Jan. 1999, p. 53.
[26] Campbell, Malcolm, "The Best Manager in America," <u>Selling Power</u>, (Jan/Feb 1999), p. 52.
[27] Lewis Eigen & Jonathan Siegel, <u>The Manager's Book of Quotations</u>, Rockville, MD, 1989, p. 25

[28] Gerstner, Louis, Who Says Elephants Can't Dance,
     (New York, 2002), p. 24.
[29] Lewis Eigen & Jonathan Siegel, The Manager's Book of Quotations,
     Rockville, MD, 1989, p. 293.
[30] Dell, Michael, Direct from Dell, (New York, 1999), p. 127.
[31] Charen, Ram and Tichy, Noel, Every Business is a Growth Business,
     (New York, 1998), p. 11.
[32] Gerstner, Louis, Who Says Elephants Can't Dance,
     (New York, 2002), p. 182.
[33] Jones, Charlie. What Makes Winners Win. Carol Publishing Group,
     (Secaucus, NJ, 1997), p.46.
[34] Gerstner, Louis, Who Says Elephants Can't Dance,
     (New York, 2002), p. 97.
[35] Walton, Sam and Huey, John. Sam Walton, Made In America.
     (NewYork, 1992), p. 128
[36] Ibid., p. 128.
[37] Ibid., p. 128.
[38] Ibid., p. 216.
[39] Slater, Robert, The Wal-Mart Decade, (New York, 2003), Front Flap
[40] Kirk Cheyfitz, Thinking Inside the Box (New York, 2003), pp. 55-56.
[41] Ibid.
[42] Ibid.
[43] Ibid.